D1564725

Mark Twain in Paradise

Mark Twain and His Circle Series

TOM QUIRK, EDITOR

Mark Twain in Paradise

His Voyages to Bermuda

Donald Hoffmann

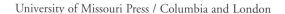

University of Missouri Press / Columbia and London

Library of Congress Cataloging-in-Publication Data

Hoffmann, Donald.
    Mark Twain in paradise : his voyages to Bermuda / Donald Hoffmann.
        p. cm. — (Mark Twain and his circle series)
    Summary: "Samuel Clemens first encountered the Bermuda Islands in
1867 and retreated there many more times for the beauty, pace, weather and
company, both local and elite. Hoffmann gathers and examines passages from
travel pieces, letters, and unpublished autobiographical dictation to illuminate
the writer's love for Bermuda and its seafaring culture"—Provided by publisher.
    Includes bibliographical references and index.
    ISBN-13: 978-0-8262-1642-7 (alk. paper)
    ISBN-10: 0-8262-1642-0 (alk. paper)
    1. Twain, Mark, 1835–1910—Travel—Bermuda Islands. 2. Authors,
American—19th century—Biography. 3. Americans—Bermuda Islands—
Biography. 4. Bermuda Islands—Biography. I. Title. II. Series.
    PS1334.H64   2006
    818'.403—dc22
                                                                    2005029153

DESIGNER: KRISTIE LEE
TYPESETTER: CRANE COMPOSITION, INC.
PRINTER AND BINDER: THOMSON-SHORE, INC.
TYPEFACE: ADOBE GARAMOND

To Alison and Michael Hoffmann

Contents

PREFACE

This study portrays both a man and a place. What took Mark Twain to Bermuda? Why did he go there so many times? How long did he stay? How did he spend his time, and with whom? What did he see? How was he received? What did he say about Bermuda?

A man and his work cannot be so easily separated, but I have tried to write of Samuel Clemens the person and Mark Twain the author and stage performer. It should also be said that the pen name, as Albert Bigelow Paine protested long ago, was Mark Twain, not "Twain." In the narrative presented here, I have favored facts, direct observation, primary sources, and various extracts in order to steer clear of secondary commentary, contrived interpretations, and the claptrap that comes from pretending to have delved successfully into someone else's unconscious. Nothing can compare with the immediacy and authenticity of Mark Twain's own words.

The task of tracking Mark Twain in Bermuda proved the wisdom of what Richard P. Feynman so happily called "the pleasure of finding things out." I am especially grateful to Patricia and L. Eugene Thomas for all their generous hospitality. I am also indebted to Karla Hayward, archivist, and her assistants Jane Downing and Richard Lowry at the Bermuda Archives, Hamilton; C. Joanne Brangman, librarian, and her staff at the Bermuda National Library, Hamilton; Dr. Wolfgang Sterrer and Penny Hill of the Bermuda Aquarium, Natural History Museum and Zoo, in Flatts; Richard D. Butterfield, the owner of Bay

House, in Pembroke Parish; Bishop Robert Kurtz of St. Theresa's Cathedral, Hamilton; and B. W. "Jordy" Walker of OBM Ltd., Hamilton.

Working with the Mark Twain Papers, in the Bancroft Library of the University of California at Berkeley, became particularly enjoyable because of the kindnesses of Robert H. Hirst, Victor Fischer, Harriet Elinor Smith, and especially Neda Salem, all of the Mark Twain Project. Elsewhere, I am indebted to my brother John Hoffmann, librarian and manuscript curator of the Illinois Historical Survey, University of Illinois Library; Alissa Rosenberg, reference librarian at the Minnesota Historical Society, in St. Paul; Joyce Wanger of the Patten Free Library, in Bath, Maine; John J. Huffman, administrator of the Mark Twain Birthplace Historic Site, in Florida, Missouri; Steven Johnson, manager of the Bronx Zoo Library, in New York; James Lewis of the New Jersey Historical Society, in Newark; Stuart Frazer of the Perry Library at Old Dominion University, in Norfolk, Virginia; Brenda Hunnicutt at the Kansas City, Missouri, Public Library; Jane McCone, former director of the Center for Mark Twain Studies at Elmira College, in Elmira, New York; Professor George Hoffmann, the University of Michigan; Professor Sarah Bradford Landau of New York University; and Professor Leonard K. Eaton of Otter Rock, Oregon. For their interest, encouragement, and help in various ways, I am grateful to Valerie Hoffmann, Eric Hoffmann, Ellen Goheen, Keith F. Davis, Gwynne Matlavage, Mary Sara Fitzgerald, Elpidio Rocha, Larry Ro-trock, and Sarah Patel.

Mark Twain in Paradise

The "Long, Strange Cruise" of 1867

Mark Twain had a magical name; Bermuda was a magical place. Mark Twain voyaged eight times to Bermuda, one of the most isolated spots in the world. All told, he spent more than six months on the Islands, a great deal of time for a man so constitutionally restless. The trips to Bermuda brought into play the basic, recurrent themes of his life and art: not only his famous humor and despair, or impulse to travel (especially on water), but also his flight from a merciless conscience, manifold ways of shading fact into fiction, and nostalgia for the long summers of a small-town childhood. Mark Twain spoke about Bermuda in his autobiographical dictations. He wrote about Bermuda in the *Atlantic Monthly* and in letters to friends both new and old. He told of the ocean vistas, the stone cottages, flowers, a certain wall, and two specimen trees—all of which can still be seen. Changes did not diminish the clean air and brilliant light, the colors of the sea, or the clear sense of a relaxed and better way of life. Mark Twain and Bermuda have thus remained inextricably linked. "You go to heaven if you want to," he wrote from the Islands in his last days. "I'd druther stay here."[1]

Samuel Langhorne Clemens first set foot in Bermuda on his return from a cruise to Europe and the Holy Land. Earlier, he had used such unpromising pen names as "Josh" and "Thomas Jefferson Snodgrass," but in February 1863 he took for a nom de guerre, as he put it, an old Mississippi River call in the shoal waters that favored boats headed upstream. It signaled a depth of two fathoms (twelve feet): safe enough for vessels of little draft, but dangerous for the largest steamboats. Hence the two-word name he chose, "Mark Twain," expressed both his affection for the river and the stresses and ambiguities of his life. It was a manly name, it caught attention like two short punches, and to Clemens himself it brought back the happy years he spent as a steamboat pilot:

When I was a boy, there was but one permanent ambition among my comrades in our village on the west bank of the Mississippi River. That was, to be a steamboatman. [FIG. I]

I loved the profession far better than any I have followed since, and I took a measureless pride in it. The reason is plain: a pilot, in those days, was the only unfettered and entirely independent human being that lived in the earth.

I was a pilot now, full fledged [by April 1859]. . . . Time drifted smoothly and prosperously on, and I supposed—and hoped—that I was going to follow the river the rest of my days, and die at the wheel when my mission was ended. But by and by the war came, commerce was suspended, my occupation was gone.[2]

FIGURE I. One permanent ambition (from *Life on the Mississippi*).

Hannibal, Missouri, where Sam Clemens was raised, was a good town to get away from and a good town to remember. "It was so quiet, so deadly quiet," he said. "Half the people were alive and the other half were dead. A stranger could not tell them apart."[3] But the sight of a steamboat brought the town suddenly to life, and travel on water, whether by raft or sail or steam, took hold of Clemens forever. He found in the nomadic instinct "a charm which, once tasted, a man will yearn to taste again."[4] If his first days in Bermuda were only incidental to a much longer voyage, on every later visit he made the Islands his only destination, and almost always traveled home refreshed.

At first an apprentice, then journeyman printer, and occasional contributor to newspapers, Clemens hoped to strike it rich in silver, or gold, or even coca. But the forces of inborn temperament and outward circumstance, he said, guided him ineluctably toward the most important aspect of his life, its literary feature. Newspapers then maintained far-flung exchanges with out-of-town papers and magazines, a mutual courtesy and lazy way of filling columns with reading matter. Such a practice led to a wide dissemination of word sketches as well as sundry items of news. Clemens held two great advantages: a seemingly innate understanding of man as the storytelling animal and a definite crankiness of mind that led him to think for himself and to express his thoughts idiosyncratically. Early in 1865, at a mining camp in Calaveras County, California, he heard a tale about a compulsive gambler who wagered on a frog well trained to outjump all others, then lost to a stranger who slyly stuffed the champion with quail shot. He fashioned a story with the title of "Jim Smiley and His Jumping Frog" and gave the name "Dan'l Webster" to the gifted frog. It was published in the November 18, 1865, issue of the *Saturday Press,* a dying New York magazine. The tale spread through the newspapers. "I published that story, & it became widely known in America, India, China, England," he wrote to a California friend in January 1870, "& the reputation it made for me has paid me thousands & thousands of dollars since."

Before he trained as a pilot, Clemens had hoped to sail to South America and journey up the Amazon. He meant to make a fortune by gathering coca leaves. His first ocean voyage, however, was devoted instead to travel writing. By then, the Civil War was over. He sailed from San Francisco in March 1866 for the Sandwich Islands, now called Hawaii. He stayed four months, and sent twenty-five letters to the *Sacramento Union.* Essentially, they were intended to encourage trade between Hawaii and California, and to promote in particular the sugar industry. Clemens amused himself with sightseeing excursions and casual sarcasms, and his letters also revealed a distaste for religion. ("I detest novels, poetry & theology," he once wrote in a notebook.) When he came upon the "meagre remains of an ancient heathen temple," he speculated about the natives of bygone days, "long, long before the missionaries braved a thousand privations to come and make them permanently miserable by telling them how beautiful and how blissful a place heaven is, and how nearly impossible it is to get there." Nor did he find the legislature any better than such bodies elsewhere. "Few men of first-class ability can afford to let their affairs go to ruin while they fool away their time in legislatures for months on a stretch," he wrote. "Few such men care a straw for the small-beer distinction one is able to achieve in such a place."[5]

His finest report to the *Union,* significantly, told the haunting story of a disaster at sea. The clipper ship *Hornet* had left New York and rounded the Horn. As it sailed toward San Francisco, on May 3, the ship caught fire. Fifteen castaways in an open boat with only ten days of provisions endured for forty-three days and eight hours before they reached Hawaii, more than thirty-three hundred miles away. Clemens, suffering from saddle boils, had himself carried to the hospital, and by listening to the survivors produced the first full account to reach the United States. When he returned to California, he wrote later, he found himself "about the best-known honest man on the Pacific Coast."[6] He sold the same story to *Harper's New Monthly Magazine,* where it appeared in the December 1866 issue. Seeing his name indexed as "Mark Swain," he thought his ambitions were sunk. "I was a Literary Person," he said, "but that was all—a buried one; buried alive."[7]

Hawaii nonetheless gave Clemens a clearer sense of a world he had only dreamed of, simple and natural and beautiful, and in Bermuda he would encounter for the second time a chain of paradise islands. Remote and unhurried places, they were happily beyond reach of the telegraph and the daily news, and were blessed with balmy weather, bright flowers, slender palm trees, and scattered white cottages fitted with green shutters. In both he found an easygoing citizenry, predominantly dark skinned and handsome.

Known already as an entertaining correspondent, Mark Twain took to the stage, an alternative way of performing with words. Orion Clemens, his older brother, said Sam had a greater capacity for both enjoyment and suffering, the temperament "to feel the utmost extreme of every feeling." Pathos resided in everything human, Mark Twain wrote later, and the secret source of humor itself was not joy, but sorrow. Clemens very much needed the sense of humor with which he was so richly endowed. His gift for telling amusing stories, moreover, made more palatable his unsparing critiques of human behavior and his conviction that man was "far and away the worst animal that exists; & the only untamable one."[8]

For his first major platform appearance, on October 2, 1866, in San Francisco, he advertised himself as the Honolulu correspondent of the *Sacramento Union,* fully prepared to discuss the Sandwich Islands and "the absurd Customs and Characteristics of the Natives." A splendid orchestra was in town, he said, "but has not been engaged." A den of ferocious wild beasts would be on exhibition "in the next Block." After other such fooleries came this: "Doors open at 7 o'clock. The Trouble to begin at 8 o'clock." Presented as a traveler and humorist, Mark Twain quickly overcame stage fright and exploited what he variously described as his sniveling drawl or drawling infirmity of speech. (Some years later, in London, a man who observed Clemens at a dinner party wrote of his "inconceivably comical drawl, which seems natural, but which one occasionally suspects is put on in order to turn over in his mind what he shall say. . . . His remarks were all shrewd, his language terse and appropriate, and his manner entirely free from affectation.")[9] After a lecture tour across California and Nevada, he pondered a grand trip around the world to generate travel letters for the San Francisco *Alta California.* Later, he abandoned the plan for a lesser voyage, a pleasure cruise organized for church people bent on seeing the Holy Land.

At thirty-one, Clemens had lived a lifetime, but now he set out to build a reputation on the East Coast. He sailed on December 15 from San Francisco, reached Nicaragua, crossed the isthmus, escaped the fatal cholera aboard ship, and arrived in New York on January 12, 1867. As he continued to post letters to the *Alta California,* he surveyed the city where he had worked in 1853, and suffered through Sundays all too quiet. "You cannot get a taste of the villainous wines and liquors of New York on the Sabbath," he wrote on February 18. "I could not even find a bootblack yesterday, or a newsboy. . . . What was left for me to do? Simply to follow the fashionable mania, and go to church. . . . They brave miles of stormy weather to worship and sing praises at the altar, and criticize each other's costumes."[10]

What seemed to him a chance to escape boring Sundays of worship, paradoxically, had already been broadcast in a prospectus that offered an "Excursion to the Holy Land, Egypt, the Crimea, Greece, and Intermediate Points of Interest." Published late in January, the program called for a stop in Bermuda on the return voyage, "and after spending a day with our friends the Bermudians, the final departure will be made for home." Prominent citizens of Brooklyn—members, mostly, of the Plymouth Church—were planning a grand pleasure trip,

Mark Twain wrote on March 2. The character and standing of every applicant, he said, "had to undergo the strictest assay by a Committee before his money would be received and his name booked." Hence his companion (the journalist Edward H. House) had introduced him, so he wrote, as the Reverend Mark Twain, of late a missionary to the Sandwich Islands. Cunning though he was, Clemens seemed not to foresee that a man who smoked, drank, swore, and played cards might not find himself at home with so many passengers who were not only older and comfortably well-to-do but also overtly pious.[11]

Mark Twain's first book, *The Celebrated Jumping Frog of Calaveras County, and Other Sketches,* appeared at the end of April. The author was already well known, his publisher announced, as the "Wild Humorist of the Pacific Slope" and the "Moralist of the Main." Notably, the sketches were advertised as representing Mark Twain in his *secondary* role, that of humorist. Clemens sent home a copy inscribed "To my mother—the dearest friend I ever had, & the truest." The book could not claim much importance, but it bolstered his status as a writer (FIG. 2). "As for the Frog book," he wrote home on June 7, "I don't believe that will ever pay anything worth a cent. I published it simply to advertise myself." He had also promoted himself by speaking about the Sandwich Islands at the Cooper Institute, on May 6. There he demonstrated a nearly perfected style, as Edward House reported:

>   The scheme of the lecturer appeared to be to employ the various facts he had gathered as bases upon which to build fanciful illustrations of character, which were furthermore embellished with a multitude of fantastic anecdotes and personal reminiscences. The frequent incongruities of the narration—evidently intentional—made it all the more diverting, and the artifice of its partial incoherence was so cleverly contrived as to intensify the amusement of the audience. . . . [H]is style is his own, and needs to be seen to be understood.[12]

To boost the Holy Land voyage, Capt. Charles C. Duncan boasted that the *Quaker City,* the ship he had leased, was "strong as an iron pot." A side-wheel steamer with auxiliary sails, it had been built in Philadelphia in 1854, and measured more than 225 feet long. Clemens thought it "a right stately-looking vessel," although he dismissed it many years later as an "excursion-tub." The *Quaker City,* bought by the U.S. Navy in 1861, survived major damage from an encounter with the Confederates near Charleston, in January 1863, and after the

FIGURE 2. The celebrated jumping frog (lecture announcement).

war was sold to private investors.[13] For the Holy Land excursion, the passenger list was expected to include Gen. William Tecumseh Sherman and the Reverend Henry Ward Beecher, pastor of the Plymouth Church in Brooklyn, and stead-fast enemy of liquor. Another of the pilgrims, the *New York Independent* reported on May 2, would be Samuel Clemens of California. He had talked the *Alta California* into paying his fare, a princely sum of $1,250, in exchange for a steady stream of travel letters. Clemens hoped, too, to gather material for a book. Never before had an American pleasure cruise set sail to cross the Atlantic.

His reporting, meantime, continued to expose the edginess of his personality, so painfully evident in a letter he wrote on June 1 to his family in St. Louis:

> It isn't any use for me to talk about the voyage, because I can have no faith in that voyage or any other voyage till the ship is under way. How do I know she will ever sail? . . .
>
> All I do know or feel, is, that I am wild with impatience to move—move—*Move!* . . . Curse the endless delays! They always kill me—they make me neglect every duty & then I have a conscience that tears me like a wild beast. I wish I never had to stop *any*where a month. I do more mean things, the moment I get a chance to fold my hands & sit down than ever I can get forgiveness for. . . .
>
> I have got a splendid, immoral, tobacco-smoking, wine-drinking, godless room-mate who is as good & true & right-minded a man as ever lived—a man whose blameless conduct & example will always be an eloquent sermon to all who shall come within their influence. But send on the professional preachers—there are none I like better to converse with—if they ain't narrow minded & bigoted they make good companions.

Less than a week later, Clemens wrote his childhood friend Will Bowen, still in Hannibal, that the Holy Land cruise was bringing together "a crowd of tiptop people," and he expected to have "a jolly, sociable, homelike trip of it for the next five or six months." But on the same day, June 7, in another letter to his family, he laid bare his ruthless conscience, an affliction he was never able to cure:

> But I am so worthless that it seems to me I never do anything or accomplish anything that lingers in my mind as a pleasant memory. My mind is stored full of unworthy conduct toward Orion & toward you all, & an accusing conscience gives me peace only in excitement & restless moving from place to place. . . .
>
> You observe that under a cheerful exterior I have got a spirit that is angry with me & gives me freely its contempt. I can get away from that at sea, & be tranquil & satisfied.

A conscience accomplished no good, he wrote later, and ranked as "one of the most disagreeable things connected with a person."[14] Outgoing and sociable, Clemens everywhere proved quick to make friends but just as loath to forgive enemies. Once, he drew up a list of persons he hated. Some he designated as permanent, and others only temporary, "to be taken up in idle moments & hated for pastime." Equally unsparing in self-criticism, he could thus excuse his mordant thoughts about mankind. "Taking myself as a just & fair *average,* & thus as being in my own person the entire human race concentrated," he wrote as if Montaigne, in a letter of November 8, 1909, "I have examined the race daily, carefully, earnestly, honestly, for 39 years—with this result: I do not think much of myself."[15]

Before the *Quaker City* sailed on June 8 the excursion party had grown smaller, the *New York Times* reported, and "not quite so select."[16] General Sherman and Henry Ward Beecher never signed on. If only by default, Mark Twain became the best-known person on board. Captain Duncan faced ocean storms and soon dropped anchor. He waited two days. At last the ship proceeded toward Horta, in the Azores, then to Gibraltar, Marseilles, Genoa, Leghorn, Naples, Palermo, Athens, Corinth, Constantinople, Sebastopol, Smyrna, Beirut, Jaffa, Alexandria, and minor points in the Mediterranean. After more than five months at sea, it arrived back in New York on November 19 (FIGS. 3 AND 4).

Clemens had rebelled at the shipboard rules. Coffee and biscuits from five to seven in the morning, lights out in staterooms by midnight—an oppressive and boring routine for a man from the world of riverboats and mining camps and reckless journalism. But the annoyances and absurdities of the pilgrimage fired his imagination. He had defied quarantine to visit the Acropolis in moonlight, had met the emperor of Russia at Yalta, and had struggled up the Great Pyramid; but he attended especially to the minor irritations of the excursion, and recorded them with zealous sarcasm. Two years later, when Mark Twain published *The Innocents Abroad, or the New Pilgrims' Progress,* his readers were treated to a broad attack against received opinion and secondhand experience. ("I offer no apologies for any departures from the usual style of travel-writing that may be charged against me," he wrote in the preface, "for I think I have seen with impartial eyes, and I am sure I have written at least honestly, whether wisely or not.") With 650 pages and more than 230 illustrations, the book stood as his first major work. Dedicated to "My Aged Mother," it achieved an immediate and lasting success.

The voyage gave Clemens grand opportunities to assail the "nauseous

FIGURE 3. Clemens in Constanti-
nople, 1867 (courtesy the Mark
Twain Project, the Bancroft
Library).

FIGURE 4. Aboard the *Quaker City;* Clemens seated behind polka-dot skirt (courtesy the Mark
Twain Project, the Bancroft Library).

sentimentality" of so much that had been said about the sights and history of the Old World.[17] At the Père-Lachaise cemetery in Paris he was impelled to discount the romance of Abelard and Héloïse, and in Milan he considered the adulation of Leonardo's mural *The Last Supper* and simply asked:

> How can they see what is not visible? What would you think of a man who looked at some decayed, blind, toothless, pock-marked Cleopatra, and said: "What matchless beauty! What soul! What expression!" What would you think of a man who gazed upon a dingy, foggy sunset, and said: "What sublimity! What feeling! What richness of coloring!" What would you think of a man who stared in ecstasy upon a desert of stumps and said: "Oh, my soul, my beating heart, what a noble forest is here!"

In rural Italy he discovered "the heart and home of priestcraft—of a happy, cheerful, contented ignorance, superstition, degradation, poverty, indolence, and everlasting unaspiring worthlessness." Despite the easy appeal of Venice, he remarked the narrow streets, the "vast, gloomy marble palaces, black with the corroding damps of centuries, and all partly submerged; no dry land visible any where, and no sidewalks worth mentioning," aspects of the city that could not stand comparison to the knowledgeable guide, who turned out to be the son of South Carolina slaves. "He reads, writes, and speaks English, Italian, Spanish, and French, with perfect facility," Mark Twain wrote. "He dresses better than any of us, I think, and is daintily polite. Negroes are deemed as good as white people, in Venice, and so this man feels no desire to go back to his native land. His judgment is correct."[18]

The prospectus had promised a brief visit with "our friends the Bermudians," a phrase Mark Twain was amused to echo three times, but to most of the pilgrims it was colored with a certain irony. They came from the North, and the British colony of Bermuda had openly sided with the South. Clemens served only two weeks as a border-state soldier in sympathy with the Confederacy, then left Missouri for the Nevada Territory in July 1861—"speedily reconstructed," his nephew wrote.[19] Moses S. Beach, one of his few friends on the Holy Land excursion, owned and edited the *New York Sun* ("The Sun Shines on All"), and reminded his readers that Bermuda became "a harbor of refuge and shelter for Confederate war steamers during our recent terrible war."[20] An agent of the Confederates in fact had been stationed in the town of St. George, where Charles M. Allen, the war consul dispatched by President Lincoln, found himself heartily unwelcome. Allen arrived in October 1861 and assumed his duties the next month. At the end of the year, he wrote to his wife:

> For some days I have been in a very unsettled state as regards to my remaining here. Everybody here thinks there is no escape from war between England and the United States. . . . The present state of things makes it very unpleasant for me here just now as there is very bitter feeling against everything and everybody belonging to the United States . . .
>
> The Military men of whom there are a great many are very busy and I am informed that they have been at work all day today making "cartridges and mounting guns." They seem to be of the opinion that our people will be after this island first thing. I told them at the dinner table today that "they need have no fear, as our people would not have such a God-forsaken place as this if they could get it for nothing."[21]

Allen soon saw the flag of the secession hoisted upon his consulate staff, and later in 1862, just before Independence Day, he found the staff itself cut down. On other occasions he was attacked in his office and on the street. He kept to his post, and eventually came to know Clemens.

The pilgrims on the *Quaker City* reached Bermuda two weeks after sailing from Madeira. They were tired and homesick. "I suppose we only stopped at the Bermudas," Mark Twain wrote, "because they were in the programme. We did not care any thing about any place at all. We wanted to go home."[22] The last stop on his long voyage figured hardly at all in *The Innocents Abroad.* Bermuda nonetheless left the same satisfying impression on Clemens as on the other passengers. In the early hours of Monday, November 11, the ship approached St. George's Island, at the East End (FIG. 5). Captain Duncan wrote in his log:

> At daylight, close in to the island, took pilot, a Negro, and passing through narrow, crooked and intricate passages with the bottom plainly in sight, entered the beautiful harbor of St. George and anchored.
>
> The pretty little town, dressed in green and white, situated on the side of a gentle hill, seemed inviting, and breakfast over, our passengers were all landed, and scattered themselves in all directions. The high hill rising from the town on which is situated the fort and telegraph was duly visited, rides and drives to Hamilton taken or organized for the morrow—

FIGURE 5. Town of St. George, about 1868, looking west (Bermuda National Trust, courtesy the Bermuda Archives).

while we (our family) contented ourselves with sailing about the charming harbor in its bright green waters and among its scores of islands. Riding, driving, walking, sailing were pleasant.

Bermuda had given us an agreeable surprise. We expected nothing but a sand hill and found high ground, green foliage and fine scenery. We were disappointed about fruit of which there is next to none, a few oranges and a few bananas being about all to be had. Everything dear—meats and fowls all received from New York or Halifax. Fish abundant at 3 pence per pound.[23]

Bermudian pilots and their ability to guide ships safely into harbor had drawn praise as well from Thomas Moore, the Irish poet and musician remembered most often for his sentimental songs ("'Tis the Last Rose of Summer") and his complicity in the burning of Lord Byron's memoirs, which Moore had previously sold for two thousand guineas to John Murray, the publisher. After a seven-day voyage from Norfolk, Virginia, the young "bard of Erin" arrived in January 1804. "Nothing can be more romantic than the little harbour of St. George," he wrote, "altogether the sweetest miniature of nature that can be imagined." Moore stayed on the Islands only a few months, just long enough to engage in several flirtations, and to pen such balmy verses as

> Floated our bark to this enchanted land,
> These leafy isles upon the ocean thrown,
> Like studs of emerald o'er a silver zone.

Andrew Marvell, in the seventeenth century, had done better:

> What should we do but sing His praise,
> That led us through the watery maze
> Unto an isle so long unknown,
> And yet far kinder than our own?[24]

With little effort, the excursionists could learn that Bermuda comprised several hundred islands, islets, and barren rocks appropriately configured as a fish-hook, tilted about forty degrees, and extended for twenty-two miles (FIG. 6). The land mass came to less than twenty square miles. Less evident, the islands described the southeastern arc of a largely submerged plateau on top of an ancient volcano. Bermuda had been shaped by windblown sand dunes of coral and other organisms that slowly consolidated through rain and decaying vegetation into limestone. Warmed by the Gulf Stream, the Islands were surrounded by the most northerly coral reefs in the Atlantic. Because of the reefs and shoals, the hurricanes and shipwrecks, Bermuda came to be known by sixteenth-century Spanish sailors as *Demoniorum Insulam,* the "Isle of Devils" (FIG. 7).[25]

The town of St. George, redolent of history, rapidly declined after the heady years of the blockade runners. It had long since lost the Royal Navy to Her Majesty's Dockyard, at the West End, and the capital to Hamilton, which was centrally situated on the mainland by Crow Lane Harbor. St. George could always take pride, however, in being the oldest settlement on the Islands, and the oldest continuously occupied town of English origin in the New World. Its story began with a "very greate storme or hurricane," as recorded by Sir George Somers, the admiral of a fleet of nine vessels dispatched from England in 1609 to relieve the famished colonists of Jamestown. The storm separated the ships. Most of them sailed on to Virginia, but the flagship *Sea Venture* took on nine feet of water before its crew discovered any leaks. Hope nearly vanished before

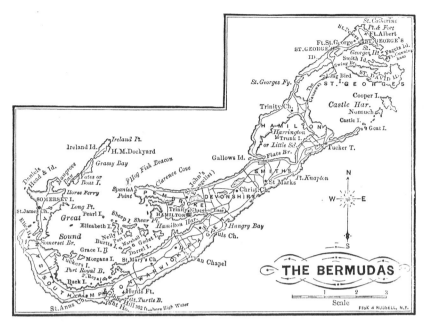

FIGURE 6. Nineteenth-century map of Bermuda (from *Harper's*, March 1874).

FIGURE 7. Rocks and boiler reefs, South Shore, Warwick Parish.

Sir George spied land on July 28. (A century earlier, about 1505, a Spanish trader named Juan de Bermudez had also seen the Islands, and they first appeared on a map in 1511, as "la bermuda.") Sir George lodged his sinking ship between two large rocks about a quarter of a mile off the East End. All 150 persons aboard survived. "Bermooda is the most plentiful place that I ever came to, for ffishe, Hogges and ffowle," Sir George gratefully reported. It was also a place "never inhabited by any christian or Heathen people," another sailor remarked. It thus became a colony without the subjugation of any aboriginals, any "Other." Bermuda had no native mammals—the "Hogges" were left by earlier castaways—and only a single endemic species of bird, the easily caught and thereby unfortunate cahow, so named in imitation of its eerie nighttime call.[26]

Word of the shipwreck reached London, and Shakespeare wrote *The Tempest.* The poet displaced his "most desolate isle" to a point between Tunis and Naples, in the Mediterranean, and peopled it with Prospero, Miranda, Ariel, and that unspeakable "thing of darkness," Caliban. At anchor in St. George's Harbor, the *Quaker City* rested far from the Mediterranean and only about 775 miles southeast of New York. When the novelist Anthony Trollope spent two dreary weeks in Bermuda in 1859 he was nevertheless moved to think of Shakespeare:

> If these be the veritable scenes of Prospero's incantations, I will at any rate say this—that there are now to be found stronger traces of the breed of Caliban than that of Ariel. Strong, however, of neither; for though Caliban did not relish working for his master more keenly than a Bermudian of the present day, there was nevertheless about him a sort of energy which is altogether wanting in the existing islanders.[27]

Two years later, the census of 1861 counted a population of 11,451, with most of the citizenry ascribed to the Church of England. Seamen outnumbered carpenters and masons, but laborers and domestic servants constituted the largest occupational groups. The telegraph station Captain Duncan saw on the hill of Fort George announced incoming ships and other news by signaling with colored flags, pennants, and hoisted balls. Other stations operated from the Dockyard and from the mainland at both the Gibbs Hill lighthouse and the governor's residence, Mount Langton.

So long at sea, and now so close to the end of the voyage, Clemens almost fell silent about his first visit to Bermuda. Others left a better record. Moses Beach, for one, found the scenery "little less than bewitching." The slow means of travel made it seem all the more luxuriant; in conveying the pilgrims off St. George's Island, the stage had to cross from Ferry Point to Coney Island and onto the mainland on a barge towed by horses. Much of the garrison had left town early in October to escape the yellow fever, and could be seen encamped at Ferry Point and on Castle Island. (A virulent and fatal fever appeared at the end of May, the consul reported, on a Spanish warship anchored near the Dock-yard.)[28] To eliminate the tedious ferry, Beach wrote, a great Causeway was planned. Construction was started on October 23, and the Causeway took four more years to finish. Another of the pilgrims, Mary Mason Fairbanks, whom Clemens fondly called "Mother Fairbanks," delighted in the town of St. George, "where the Consul resides." It had a beautiful neatness, she reported in the *Cleveland Herald*, a paper edited by her husband, because the houses "being altogether of soft stone, were painted white, and the roofs all whitewashed" (FIG. 8). Writing as "Myra," she also told of a species of palm "whose tall and naked trunks looked like granite columns, the ruins of some ancient corridor."[29]

Mrs. Fairbanks and her party followed the North Shore Road and enjoyed

FIGURE 8. Old house on St. David's Island, St. George's Parish.

the vistas toward Ireland Island and the Dockyard. They reached Hamilton in time for the midday meal, and registered at the only hotel shown on a map published a few years later (FIGS. 9 AND 10). Construction of the Hamilton Hotel by the city had commenced as early as 1852, but the building only gradually attained much size. It perched above the harbor "like a citadel," Mrs. Fairbanks wrote. (On the site today stands the city hall.) They met W. C. J. Hyland, a fellow Christian and eminent citizen of St. George, where he founded the YMCA and ran the Sunday school. Hyland, who once took in Consul Allen as a boarder, was also a magistrate, justice of the peace, and shipper. His wife had come from Brooklyn, and they lived at Caledonia Park, an imposing house at 4 Cut Road, high above St. George's Harbor. Later, the excursionists walked around Hamilton and shopped along Front Street (FIG. 11). At evening, they chanced upon a wedding in the Wesleyan Chapel, at the head of Queen Street, and were amused to watch a "gigantic colored woman," the slow-moving sexton, nonchalantly lighting the lamps from a stepladder well after the ceremony had begun. They also witnessed the arrival of his excellency the governor, commander in chief Sir Frederick Chapman, who wore white gloves.

Tuesday morning, November 12, they rode to the Gibbs Hill lighthouse (FIG. 12). This notable structure of 1844–1846, still in use, was built largely from cast-iron parts prefabricated in England, the second such lighthouse in the world. George Grove, later renowned for his *Dictionary of Music and Musicians,* supervised the construction.[30] All in all, Mrs. Fairbanks found Bermuda a beautiful oasis. Yet she worried that the Islands lacked productivity because the colored population so outnumbered the white. Much like Trollope, she wrote:

> A few years of energetic American persevering labor, such as clears our Western wilds, would make an Eden of the Bermudas, and secure a yield of grain and fruits that would pay rich tribute to their government. The present inhabitants are content to subsist on the natural productions of the islands, but hard or systematic labor is not one of the cardinal principles of their creed. If England would give us these coral reefs, I am sure we would make of them one of the most charming resorts in the world.

Her account was echoed in a journal kept by Emily Severance, another citizen of Cleveland. Mrs. Severance wrote that her husband, Solon, took his breakfast Monday morning on the ship before going ashore with Charlie Langdon to secure carriages for the ride to Hamilton. Clemens called Charlie "the Cub" be-

FIGURE 9. Hamilton, about 1868, looking west (Bermuda National Trust, courtesy the Bermuda Archives).

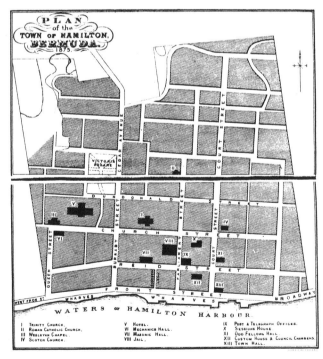

FIGURE 10. Plan of Hamilton, 1875 (courtesy the Bermuda Archives).

FIGURE 11. Front Street, Hamilton, about 1868, looking east (Bermuda National Trust, courtesy the Bermuda Archives).

cause he had just turned eighteen on August 13; early the next month, Clemens recounted much later, he stepped into Charlie's stateroom when the ship was at anchor in the Bay of Smyrna and saw on the table a likeness of Charlie's sister Olivia, whom he later met and courted and married. After months at sea, Charlie could feel more at home in St. George. The beleaguered American consul, who had come from Belmont, New York, was an old friend of Charlie's family in Elmira; and Charlie's cousin Julia Louise Langdon, also from Belmont, was visiting in Bermuda. She in fact joined the pilgrims for the journey back to New York.[31]

Mrs. Severance noted the principal buildings of Hamilton, and particularly admired a house on the west side of Queen Street. Just outside the town limit, the place was thus known as Par-la-Ville. It belonged to William B. Perot, the first postmaster of Hamilton. In 1848 he issued the first Bermuda stamp. Mrs. Severance wrote of an immense Indian rubber tree (*Ficus elastica*) in front of Perot's house (FIG. 13). Sent to Hamilton from the British colony of Guiana, in South America, it had been transplanted twenty years earlier. (Somewhat reduced by storms, the tree survives today as a town landmark.) After the excur-

FIGURE 12. Gibbs Hill lighthouse, Southampton Parish.

sion Tuesday morning to the Gibbs Hill lighthouse, the party dined again at the Hamilton Hotel, and returned to St. George's to prepare for an evening at the home of Mr. and Mrs. Hyland. Busy though he was, Hyland kept a diary in which he made brief entries about the weather and ship arrivals, sometimes ornamenting them with tiny sketches of the vessels. When he turned fifty, on September 6, he looked back on his early years of "wilfulness and disobedience," and declared he was ashamed of himself. Clearly, he did not take to Clemens— whose name he misspelled and listed last among the guests that night: "Entertained Mrs. Fairbanks, Mr. and Mrs. Severance, Mr. Langdon, Moses S. Beach

FIGURE 13. Indian rubber tree, Queen Street, Hamilton (Coit album, courtesy the Bermuda Archives).

and daughter, and Mr. Clements ('Mark Twain'). Weather exhibiting change at night. Wind Westerly."[32]

At midnight they all headed back toward the ship. Mrs. Fairbanks reported in the *Herald:*

> Our steamer was anchored about a mile from shore. The wind had risen, and in putting off from shore, we soon experienced much difficulty in stemming the current. Our oarsmen tugged manfully, and "Mark Twain" held the rudder with a strong hand, while the spray dashed over his Parisian broadcloth and almost extinguished his inevitable cigar. For a time it seemed as if the longer we sailed, the farther we drifted from the lights of the *Quaker City,* and I flung my cloak over my face to shut out the dark ocean that stretched beyond us. At length human strength prevailed over the elements.

The *Bermuda Royal Gazette,* then a weekly paper of slight size and little content, reported on Tuesday that Captain Duncan and his sixty-three excursionists, including Daniel D. Leary, one of the owners of the ship, had arrived the day before. "No deaths since leaving the United States," the newspaper said. The *Colonist,* a rival paper, printed a formal list of the pilgrims as a souvenir. A gale struck the Islands on Wednesday, November 13. "Weather squally. Wind N.W.," Hyland noted in his diary. He gallantly carried flowers aboard the ship, but seemed not to have appreciated the stay of Charlie Langdon's cousin. "Miss Langdon took her departure," he wrote, "and went on board the *Quaker City* for New York much to my gratification." Stormy weather continued Thursday morning, when the ship was to have sailed. Hyland and his wife, Mary, entertained two more of the excursionists, Dr. and Mrs. James H. Payne of Boston. Finally, the pilgrims sailed on Friday morning, November 15. The next issue of the *Royal Gazette* reported they had been delighted with the Islands.

The ship reached New York on November 19. Mark Twain unburdened himself by writing of the "long, strange cruise" that had "not blackguards enough on board in proportion to the saints." In turn, one of the pilgrims kept a journal in which he described Clemens as "a wicked fellow that will take the name of the Lord in vain, that is no respecter of persons, yet he is liberal, kind and obliging, and if he were only a Christian would make his mark." Clemens said he was able to make good friends of only eight or nine of the pilgrims: "Three-fourths of the *Quaker City*'s passengers were between forty and seventy years of age! There was a picnic crowd for you! . . . The venerable excursionists were not gay and frisky. . . . They never romped, they talked but little, they never sang, save in the nightly prayer-meeting. The pleasure ship was a synagogue, and the pleasure trip was a funeral excursion without a corpse."[33]

The great Holy Land excursion of 1867 had taken Clemens for the first time to the Old World. For the first time, if only in a miniature portrait, he saw Olivia Langdon. The tour also resulted in his first substantial work: a book, he said, that made him "profitably notorious all over America." Despite the annoyances, there were good moments and good friendships. Clemens could also harbor kind thoughts about Bermuda:

> Days passed—and nights; and then the beautiful Bermudas rose out of the sea, we entered the tortuous channel, steamed hither and thither among the bright summer islands, and rested at last under the flag of England and were welcome. We were not a nightmare here, where were civilization and intelligence in place of Spanish and Italian superstition, dirt and dread of cholera. A few days among the breezy groves, the flower gardens, the coral caves, and the lovely vistas of blue water that went

curving in and out, disappearing and anon again appearing through jungle walls of brilliant foliage, restored the energies dulled by long drowsing on the ocean, and fitted us for our final cruise—our little run of a thousand miles to New York—America—HOME.

We bade good-bye to "our friends the Bermudians," as our programme hath it—the majority of those we were most intimate with were negroes—and courted the great deep again. I said the majority. We knew more negroes than white people, because we had a deal of washing to be done, but we made some excellent friends among the whites, whom it will be a pleasant duty to hold long in grateful remembrance.[34]

II

An Idle Excursion in 1877

Two days after he returned, Clemens left New York to work in Washington, D.C. He still grumbled about the "strange menagerie of ignorance, imbecility, bigotry & dotage" aboard the *Quaker City*.[1] The long voyage, moreover, had left him as restless as ever. He was already dead-tired of being in one place so long, he said on December 13, and might soon grow disgusted and sail for California. The day before Christmas, he wrote to Emily Severance, his shipboard friend. "I am in a fidget to move," Clemens said. "It isn't a novel sensation, though—I never was any other way."

Nearly ten years went by before Mark Twain wrote about Bermuda again. By the end of 1876, he had published *The Adventures of Tom Sawyer,* had begun the long process of writing the *Adventures of Huckleberry Finn,* and was at work with Bret Harte on a stage play titled *Ah Sin,* a potboiler drawn from the stereotype of a Chinese laundryman. The early months of 1877 exhausted him. He revised the play, rehearsed it in Baltimore, and quarreled not only with Harte, a notorious drinker and shameless sponger, but also with Captain Duncan, who was still giving lectures about the voyage of the *Quaker City.* Clemens returned to his home in Hartford, Connecticut, on May 1. He took to bed with a cold and with what he called his pet devil, bronchitis. Illness kept him from Washington and the opening of the play on May 7. After deciding to sail to Bermuda, he had cards printed to say that "Mr. Clemens has gone away on a sea voyage of uncertain duration, but will answer your letter as soon as he returns to this country." He mailed one to his brother Orion, by now in Keokuk, Iowa. "Profanity is more necessary to me than is immunity from colds," Clemens scribbled across it, adding that death would be preferable to the remedy Orion had suggested.

Clemens also wanted to escape from his "trained Presbyterian conscience," that unwitting gift from the dearest friend he ever had, his mother. "I am going off on a sea voyage," he wrote to Sue Crane, his sister-in-law. "It is to get the world & the devil out of my head." With reason or not, Clemens habitually felt ashamed of himself, and he would make Huck Finn denounce the nature of guilt: "But that's always the way; it don't make no difference whether you do right or wrong, a person's conscience ain't got no sense, and just goes for him *anyway.* If I had a yaller dog that didn't know no more than a person's conscience does, I would pison him. It takes up more room than all the rest of a person's insides, and yet ain't no good, nohow." Clemens held conscience to be a malignant invention, a pitiless enemy that ruled as if an "insolent absolute Monarch inside of a man."[2]

His memories of a boy's life on the Mississippi held the peculiar charm that had colored his entire career. Bermuda was another idyllic place, full of peace and quiet, like his bygone summers in Hannibal. The voyage in itself could provide the sense of enlarged freedom that soon became the manifold theme of his masterwork, *Adventures of Huckleberry Finn:* the freedom from slavery, from the genteel, the indoors, and all "the bars and shackles of civilization." Simply to glide on a raft, Mark Twain would write in *A Tramp Abroad,* surpassed walking in the heat of the day, or tedious jolting behind tired horses, or the rush of railroad cars—for it "calms down all feverish activities, it soothes to sleep all nervous hurry and impatience; under its restful influence all the troubles and vexations and sorrows that harass the mind vanish away, and existence becomes a dream, a charm, a deep and tranquil ecstasy." Springtime, finally, was the season of vague longings, of "dreams of flight to peaceful islands in the remote solitudes of the sea."[3]

He delayed the voyage for a week to accommodate his companion, the Reverend Joseph H. Twichell. In befriending Twichell for more than forty years, Clemens gave proof to his comment that professional preachers, if not narrow-minded and bigoted, made excellent company. When they first met, in the fall of 1868, Twichell already was the pastor of the Asylum Hill Congregational Church, in Hartford, and Clemens was staying across from the church at the home of his publisher, Elisha Bliss. Twichell understood that in traveling with

Mark Twain he might be caricatured later as a bumpkin or fool. He also knew that his friend's commentaries on life would reach well beyond the pale and pieties of religion. But the reverend chose not to resist what he described as "the brightness of his mind, the incomparable charm of his talk, and his rare companionableness."[4] Early in 1870 he officiated at Clemens's wedding, and in 1874 he and Clemens attempted to hike from Hartford to Boston. It was for Twichell, again, that Mark Twain wrote his clandestine and naughty manuscript titled "*Date 1601. Conversation, as it was by the Social Fireside, in the time of the Tudors*"—evidence enough that the reverend was hardly narrow-minded. Clemens said he found it heartbreakingly dreary to travel alone, and was pleased with Twichell's intelligent conversation and his "patience and endurance, two good ingredients for a man travelling with me."[5]

When they left Hartford for the voyage, Clemens took along his notebook. "First actual pleasure trip I ever took," he wrote, "a recreation trip . . . a *relaxation* trip." Yet the number of notes he made quickly belied his words. An ambitious writer never stops working. The two friends left New Haven on a boat not long before midnight on Wednesday, May 16. In New York the next morning Clemens already began to poke fun of his companion. "Joe & I have been wandering about for half an hour with satchells & overcoats," he wrote to his wife, Livy, "asking questions of policemen; at last we have found the eating house I was after. Joe's country aspect & the seal-skin coat [on Clemens] caused one policeman to follow us a few blocks. . . . I judge we are 'shadowed' & shall be in the station house presently." The café in question stood on William Street near Fulton. At breakfast, Clemens tried to impress upon the waiter that he was in the company of a minister, then realized that Twichell "didn't look clerical."[6]

Clemens was paying Twichell's passage and all of his expenses. They sailed from New York that afternoon in first class, on the mail steamer *Bermuda*. The ship carried only thirteen other passengers. Few tourists from the East Coast ventured to Bermuda in the years following the Civil War. If they knew so little about the Islands, it was because the lack of a regular steamer schedule kept them from learning anything more. Before 1873, when Bermuda began to subsidize the Quebec S.S. Company and its mail steamer *Canima,* the average number of first-class adult passengers on ships from New York to Bermuda amounted to only ten. The *Canima* was certified for forty passengers. It was joined in 1875 by a second ship, the *Bermuda*.[7] No one reading Trollope, however, would have been encouraged to visit the Islands. He boarded a steamer that ran to Bermuda only once a month from St. Thomas, in the Virgin Islands.

The ship took four days to reach St. George's Harbor. "Looking back at my fortnight's sojourn," Trollope wrote, "it seems to me that there can be no place in the world as to which there can be less to be said than there is about this island." After a week in St. George and another week in Hamilton, he could not bring himself to declare which was "the most triste." The soil of the Islands appeared fertile but was poorly cultivated. He saw no vegetables except potatoes and onions. His meals looked hardly fit to eat. The climate in late May and early June was muggy and disagreeable, and the people seemed only half awake—an observation that later visitors would sometimes echo:

> The sleepiness of the people appeared to me the most prevailing characteristic of the place. . . . To say that they live for eating and drinking would be to wrong them. They want the energy for the gratification of such vicious tastes. To live and die would seem to be enough for them. To live and die as their fathers and mothers did before them, in the same houses, using the same furniture, nurtured on the same food, and enjoying the same immunity from the dangers of excitement.[8]

Bermuda was further maligned in October 1873 in an unsigned commentary in *Harper's Weekly*. The fishhook-like Islands perhaps were supported only on a coral stem or pillar, the magazine said, that might well be torpedoed. Winter gales from the northwest wreaked great damage to ships, and thus demonstrated the justice of Shakespeare's epithet, "the still-vex'd Bermoothes." Soldiers dispatched to the Islands soon found the work hard and the climate like a Turkish bath. Drunkenness and suicide were "fearfully rife." Europeans typically broke down after a year or two, the magazine continued, "not from actual illness, but from sheer weakness and exhaustion."[9]

A retraction appeared only a few weeks later. Bermuda now was pronounced "a delightful place of resort during the winter season." To make further amends, *Harper's New Monthly Magazine* for March 1874 gave seventeen pages to the Islands—"so strangely unfamiliar to most well-informed Americans." Cited among the many pleasures were the roads and vistas; an agreeable climate especially beneficial for those afflicted by rheumatism, bronchitis, and nervous diseases; a polite citizenry, whose manners—particularly, those of the women—had a "simplicity almost Arcadian"; clean air, sometimes deliciously laden with "the perfumes of the flowers"; and all the amusements, such as driving, rowing, yachting, cricket, croquet, dinner parties, and hotel dances. Bermuda, finally, was described as a paradise for naturalists.[10]

By the spring of 1877, when Clemens and Twichell set sail, Bermuda had not yet become a delightful place of resort for large numbers of Americans. Moreover, by May the season had ended. Clemens nevertheless "shipped in the name of Langhorne (his middle name)," Twichell wrote in his journal. At forty-one, Mark Twain chose to travel largely incognito. He was already widely known from his platform performances and books. After *The Innocents Abroad* he had published *Roughing It* and a novel titled *The Gilded Age,* written with Charles Dudley Warner; a collection of short pieces, *Sketches, New and Old,* and *The Adventures of Tom Sawyer.* Although it was many years later that Archibald Henderson pronounced him "the greatest genius evolved by natural selection out of the ranks of American journalism," Mark Twain in 1877 was well on his way toward becoming the best-known storyteller in the world—an amazing achievement for an impish, unregenerate river-town boy always called "Youth" by his wife.[11]

Once again, Clemens stayed only four days on the Islands, and two were rainy. But he compiled enough notes from the "pleasure trip" to generate four articles for the *Atlantic Monthly.* After deliberation, he titled his series "Some Rambling Notes of an Idle Excursion." He began with more than twenty paragraphs that failed to disclose where he and the reverend were headed:[12]

All the journeyings I had ever done had been purely in the way of business. The pleasant May weather suggested a novelty, namely, a trip for pure recreation, the bread-and-butter element left out. The Reverend said he would go, too: a good man, one of the best of men, although a clergyman. By eleven at night we were in New Haven and on board the New York boat. We bought our tickets, and then went wandering around, here and there, in the solid comfort of being free and idle, and of putting distance between ourselves and the mails and telegraphs.

After a while I went to my state-room and undressed, but the night was too enticing for bed. We were moving down the bay now, and it was pleasant to stand at the window and take the cool night-breeze and watch the gliding lights on shore. . . .

The next day, in New York, was a hot one. . . . Toward the middle of the afternoon we arrived on board the stanch steamship Bermuda, with bag and baggage, and hunted for a shady place. . . .

By nightfall we were far out at sea, with no land in sight. No telegrams could come here, no letters, no news. This was an uplifting thought. It was still more uplifting to reflect that the millions of harassed people on shore behind us were suffering just as usual.

The next day [Friday, May 18] brought us into the midst of the Atlantic solitudes,—out of smoke-colored soundings into the fathomless deep blue; no ships visible anywhere over the wide ocean; no company but Mother Cary's chickens wheeling, darting, skimming the waves in the sun.

He had described the darting petrels in his notebook as "very beautiful; bronze, shiny, metallic, broad white stripe across tail." They were "supposed to sleep on the water at night," he wrote. It was six o'clock in the morning on Whitsunday, May 20, when the *Bermuda* made land, but in the "Idle Excursion" he altered the hour:

At eight o'clock on the third morning out from New York, land was sighted. Away across the sunny waves one saw a faint dark stripe stretched along under the horizon,—or pretended to see it, for the credit of his eyesight. Even the Reverend said he saw it, a thing which was manifestly not so. But I never have seen anyone who was morally strong enough to confess that he could not see land when others claimed that they could.

By and by the Bermuda Islands were easily visible. The principal one lay upon the water in the distance, a long, dull-colored body, scalloped with slight hills and valleys. We could not go straight at it, but had to travel all the way around it, sixteen miles from shore, because it is fenced with an invisible coral reef. At last we sighted buoys, bobbing here and there, and then we glided into a narrow channel among them, "raised the reef," and came upon shoaling blue water that soon further shoaled into pale green, with a surface scarcely rippled.

The ship had sailed through the North Channel to the East End, where it entered the Narrows Channel by the coast of St. George's Island, close to the shoals where the *Sea Venture* wrecked. It turned back along the North Shore to Grassy Bay, and entered the Great Sound. After passing islands large and small (a scene, later, that Lady Brassey thought "very Norwegian in character"), the *Bermuda* approached Hamilton Harbor by slipping between Hinson's Island and Marshall's Island, an opening known as Timlins' Narrows:[13]

We followed the narrow channel a long time, with land on both sides,— low hills that might have been green and grassy, but had a faded look instead. However, the land-locked water was lovely, at any rate, with its glittering belts of blue and green where moderate soundings were, and its broad splotches of rich brown where the rocks lay near the surface. . . .

At last we steamed between two island points whose rocky jaws allowed only just enough room for the vessel's body, and now before us loomed Hamilton on her clustered hillsides and summits, the whitest mass of terraced architecture that exists in the world, perhaps. . . .

So the Reverend and I had at last arrived at Hamilton, the principal town in the Bermuda Islands. A wonderfully white town; white as snow itself. White as marble; white as flour. Yet looking like none of these, exactly. Never mind, we said; we shall hit upon a figure by and by that will describe this peculiar white.

It was a town that was compacted together upon the sides and tops of a cluster of small hills. Its outlying borders fringed off and thinned away among the cedar forests, and there was no woody distance of curving coast, or leafy islet sleeping upon the dimpled, painted sea, but was flecked with shining white points—half-concealed houses peeping out of the foliage. The architecture of the town was mainly Spanish, inherited from the colonists of two hundred and fifty years ago. Some ragged-topped cocoa-palms, glimpsed here and there, gave the land a tropical aspect.

Trollope had also thought of snow when he saw Bermuda. "Every house is white, up from the ground to the very point of the roof," he wrote. "Nothing is in so great demand as whitewash. They whitewash their houses incessantly, and always include the roofs." He found the effect painful to his eyes. Clemens wrote in his notebook: "Houses painfully white—town & houses & verandahs all Spanish style." But the settlers were British, not Spanish, and the style of the cottages, akin to that of houses in rural England, responded more directly to the local environment. Clemens perhaps recalled the white buildings he had seen in Spain, or the article in *Harper's Monthly,* which said the spirit of old Juan Bermudez seemed to float over the Islands—"so thoroughly Spanish are the outward characteristics." In 1883, a correspondent for the *New York Times* could still puzzle over St. George. It was so much like an old Spanish town, he wrote, "it seemed odd to hear the people talking English"; and in 1890, a popular guide-book referred to "the white gleam of the Spanish looking houses." Trollope real-ized that Bermuda was "so circumstanced geographically that it should be the early market-garden for New York—as to a certain small extent it is."[14] When the *Bermuda* returned to New York, it carried a cargo of 13,464 boxes of onions, 3,010 barrels of potatoes, and 11,397 boxes and 97 crates of tomatoes. The time for shipping Easter lilies had passed (FIG. 14). Onions, most of all, advertised Bermuda. (By happy coincidence, not contrivance, the most distinguished twentieth-century architect on the Islands was named Wilfred Onions.) Farmers planted imported seeds in the small valleys of reddish, fertile soil. Blessed with a mild and moist climate, they raised onions that looked cleaner and tasted sweeter than the usual American produce. Bermuda became known as the "Onion Patch," and Bermudians, much to Mark Twain's amusement, were called "onions":

FIGURE 14. Field of Easter lilies, about 1910.

There was an ample pier of heavy masonry; upon this, under shelter, were some thousands of barrels containing that product which has carried the fame of Bermuda to many lands, the potato. With here and there an onion. That last sentence is facetious; for they grow at least two onions in Bermuda to one potato. The onion is the pride and joy of Bermuda. It is her jewel, her gem of gems. In her conversation, her pulpit, her literature, it is her most frequent and eloquent figure. In Bermudian metaphor it stands for perfection,—perfection absolute.

The Bermudian weeping over the departed exhausts praise when he says, "He was an onion!" The Bermudian extolling the living hero bankrupts applause when he says, "He is an onion!" The Bermudian setting his son upon the stage of life to dare and to do for himself climaxes all counsel, supplication, admonition, comprehends all ambition, when he says, "Be an onion!"[15]

When parallel with the pier, and ten or fifteen steps outside it, we anchored. It was Sunday, bright and sunny. The groups upon the pier— men, youths, and boys—were whites and blacks in about equal proportion. All were well and neatly dressed, many of them nattily, a few of them very stylishly. One would have to travel far before he would find another town of twelve thousand inhabitants that could represent itself so respectably, in the matter of clothes, on a freight-pier, without premeditation or effort.

Clemens had confused the population of Hamilton, which *Harper's Monthly* estimated at no more than 2,000, with the entire population of the Islands, given in the census of 1871 as 12,121. Nor were the races equally divided; the census showed 7,396 colored persons and 4,725 whites:

The women and young girls, black and white, who occasionally passed by, were nicely clad, and many were elegantly and fashionably so. The men did not affect summer clothing much, but the girls and women did, and their white garments were good to look at, after so many months of familiarity with sombre colors.

Around one isolated potato barrel stood four young gentlemen, two black, two white, becomingly dressed, each with the head of a slender cane pressed against his teeth, and each with a foot propped up on the barrel. Another young gentleman came up, looked longingly at the barrel, but saw no rest for his foot there, and turned pensively away to seek another barrel. . . . Nobody sat upon a barrel, as is the custom of the idle in other lands, yet all the isolated barrels were humanly occupied. . . . The habits of all peoples are determined by their circumstances. The Bermudians lean upon barrels because of the scarcity of lamp-posts.

In the Holy Land the pilgrims of the *Quaker City* excursion had been "assailed by a clamorous army of donkey-drivers, guides, peddlers and beggars," Mark Twain wrote, and at the Great Pyramid they were met by a rabble of Arabs who "thrust their services upon us uninvited."[16] Hence he appreciated not being harassed in Bermuda:

We went ashore and found a novelty of a pleasant nature: there were no hackmen, hacks, or omnibuses on the pier or about it anywhere, and nobody offered his services to us, or molested us in any way. I said it was like being in heaven. The Reverend rebukingly and rather pointedly advised me to make the most of it, then. We knew of a boarding-house, and what we needed now was somebody to pilot us to it. Presently a little barefooted colored boy came along, whose raggedness was conspicuously un-Bermudian. His rear was so marvelously bepatched with colored squares and triangles that one was half persuaded he had got it out of an atlas. When the sun struck him right, he was as good to follow as a lightning-bug. We hired him and dropped into his wake. He piloted us through one picturesque street after another, and in due course deposited us where we belonged. He charged nothing for his map, and but a trifle for his services; so the Reverend doubled it. The little chap received the money with a beaming applause in his eye which plainly said, "This man's an onion!"

In truth, they had planned to stay at the Hamilton Hotel, which was advertised in the *Bermuda Pocket Almanack* as newly expanded to one hundred guest rooms. The rooms cost $2.50 a night. But the season was over and the hotel had closed. Not many American tourists cared to stay in Bermuda after the first of May, the *New York Times* reported a few years later, for by then "the weather is good enough at home."[17] The little barefoot guide could easily have reminded

Clemens of his childhood (FIG. 15). He took them past the hotel and to Cedar Avenue, the northward extension of Burnaby Street, where a long vault of darkling trees was counted among the tourist sights of Hamilton (FIG. 16). They stopped at a place advertised in the *Royal Gazette* as "Mrs. Kirkham's Private Boarding House," and Clemens was pleased. He had led a vagabond, boardinghouse life before he married Livy and discovered that her father, a man of great wealth, had given them a furnished house on Delaware Avenue in Buffalo, New York, complete with servants. A few years later, Clemens built an extravagant house of his own, in Hartford. But a house effectively anchored him, Clemens said, and attracted a bothersome volume of mail. To his friend William Dean Howells, the novelist, editor, and critic, he once confided how much he would enjoy the occasional release from "housekeeping slavery" to wild independence. "A life of don't-care-a-damn in a boarding house," Clemens wrote, "is what I have asked for in many a secret prayer."[18]

Mary Ann Kirkham, a widow, ran the boardinghouse with her daughter Emily, and talked about onions as if they were sacred. Twichell wrote later that

FIGURE 15. "Chums," about 1910.

FIGURE 16. Cedar Avenue, Hamilton, 1890 (Plimpton album, courtesy the Bermuda Archives).

they were the only guests, but Mark Twain whimsically veered from fact and pretended they were lucky to be received:

> We had brought no letters of introduction; our names had been misspelt in the passenger list; nobody knew whether we were honest folk or otherwise. So we were expecting to have a good private time in case there was nothing in our general aspect to close boarding-house doors against us. We had no trouble. Bermuda has had but little experience of rascals, and is not suspicious. We got large, cool, well-lighted rooms on a second floor, overlooking a bloomy display of flowers and flowering shrubs,—calla and annunciation lilies, lantanas, heliotrope, jessamine, roses, pinks, double geraniums, oleanders, pomegranates, blue morning-glories of a great size, and many plants that were unknown to me.

Sunday afternoon they began to explore Bermuda on foot. Clemens paid special attention to the houses and their "coral" structure, although Bermuda limestone has only a small content of coral:

> We took a long afternoon walk and soon found out that that exceedingly white town was built of blocks of white coral. Bermuda is a coral island, with a six-inch crust of soil on top of it, and every man has a quarry on

his own premises. Everywhere you go you see square recesses cut into the hillsides, with perpendicular walls unmarred by crack or crevice, and perhaps you fancy that a house grew out of the ground there, and had been removed in a single piece from the mould. If you do, you err. But the material for a house has been quarried there. They cut right down through the coral, to any depth that is convenient,—ten to twenty feet,—and take it out in great square blocks [FIG. 17]. This cutting is done with a chisel that has a handle twelve or fifteen feet long, and is used as one uses a crowbar when he is drilling a hole, or a dasher when he is churning. Thus soft is this stone. Then with a common handsaw they saw the great blocks into handsome, huge bricks that are two feet long, a foot wide, and about six inches thick. These stand loosely piled during a month to harden; then the work of building begins.

They came to a new house on a rocky point, and were told that the house and site cost only $900—"probably a lie," Clemens wrote in his notes. He estimated

FIGURE 17. Stone quarry, about 1910.

that the house alone would cost $10,000 to $15,000 in New England or New York. They also saw two new cottages said to cost $480 each—"another lie."[19] Mark Twain continued:

      The house is built of these blocks; it is roofed with broad coral slabs an inch thick, whose edges lap upon each other, so that the roof looks like a succession of shallow steps or terraces; the chimneys are built of the coral blocks, and sawed into graceful and picturesque patterns; the ground-floor veranda is paved with coral blocks; also the walk to the gate; the fence is built of coral blocks,—built in massive panels, with broad cap-stones and heavy gate-posts, and the whole trimmed into easy lines and comely shape with the saw [FIG. 18].

Clemens had a good eye for architectural construction and style, and he believed circumstance to be man's master. Still, he failed to observe that nearly every important characteristic of the traditional Bermuda cottage answered directly to natural conditions.[20] Exposed to brilliant sunlight, high humidity, salt air, heavy rains, high winds, and occasional hurricanes, all of which could assault its fabric and render the interior disagreeable if not dangerous, the vernacular house was built as a barrier against the elements. It became a mass of stuccoed stone walls below a terraced roof of stone tiles. Stone chimneys and occasional stone buttresses countered the thrust from the roof load, and helped to anchor the whole to its rocky site. Mark Twain, again:

      Then they put a hard coat of whitewash, as thick as your thumb nail, on the fence and all over the house, roof, chimneys, and all; the sun comes out and shines on this spectacle, and it is time for you to shut your unaccustomed eyes, lest they be put out. It is the whitest white you can conceive of, and the blindingest. . . . It is exactly the white of the icing of a cake, and has the same unemphasized and scarcely perceptible polish.

In the absence of freshwater streams or springs, Bermudians depended on rainwater collected on the roofs and guided by gutter stones to drain pipes and down into large cisterns. Known simply as tanks, the cisterns were usually built underground. Clemens alluded to the custom only in his notebook. He became preoccupied by all the whiteness, designed to reflect the heat of the sun:

FIGURE 18. House on Chapel Lane, town of St. George.

After the house is cased in its hard scale of white-wash, not a crack, or sign of a seam, or joining of the blocks is detectable, from base-stone to chimney-top; the building looks as if it had been carved from a single block of stone, and the doors and windows sawed out afterwards. A white marble house has a cold, tomb-like, unsociable look, and takes the conversation out of a body and depresses him. Not so with a Bermuda house. There is something exhilarating, even hilarious, about its vivid whiteness when the sun plays upon it. If it be of picturesque shape and graceful contour,—and many of the Bermudian dwellings are,—it will so fascinate you that you will keep your eyes on it until they ache.

One of those clean-cut, fanciful chimneys,—too pure and white for this world,—with one side glowing in the sun and the other touched with a soft shadow, is an object that will charm one's gaze by the hour. I know of no other country that has chimneys worthy to be gazed at and gloated over [FIG. 19].

Wherever you go, in town or country, you find those snowy houses, and always with masses of bright-colored flowers about them. . . . Wherever you go, in the town or along country roads, among little potato farms and patches or expensive country-seats, these stainless white dwellings, gleaming out from flowers and foliage, meet you at every turn. The least little bit of a cottage is as white and blemishless as the stateliest mansion. . . . The roads, the streets, the dwellings, the people, the clothes,—this neatness extends to everything that falls under the eye. It is the tidiest country in the world. And very much the tidiest, too. . . .

What a bright and startling spectacle one of those blazing white country palaces, with its brown-tinted window caps and ledges, and green shutters, and its wealth of caressing flowers and foliage, would be in black London! And what a gleaming surprise it would be in nearly any American city one could mention, too![21]

In all he wrote about the traditional Bermuda cottage, Mark Twain left untouched the aspect of floor plans, which were typically extended for better ventilation (FIG. 20). The roof, thereby expanded, caught more rainwater. Sometimes, the principal floor was elevated to escape the dampness of a ground floor. A raised floor also caught more breeze, and gained better views toward the water. Similarly, the principal rooms featured "tray" ceilings, so named because as they reached into the slope of a hipped roof they remained flat, and thus looked like huge upside-down trays. Such ceilings accommodated warm air, aided ventilation, and enhanced interior spaciousness. (The collar ties between rafters came not at the wall plate, where most efficient, but a third of the way or halfway up toward the ridge board.) Often, the ground story or basement was set into a hillside. It comprised lesser apartments, storage areas, and utility rooms. In bygone

FIGURE 19. Chimney, town of St. George.

FIGURE 20. Plan of an early cottage, Warwick Parish (from John S. Humphreys, *Bermuda Houses*).

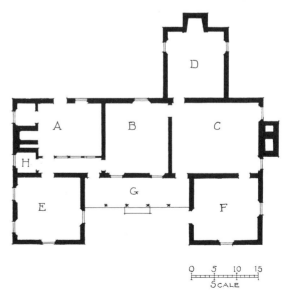

times, the ground story embraced slave quarters—sometimes outfitted with leg irons—and stables. But slavery had been ended in 1834.

Mark Twain turned instead to the roads, as yet unpaved:

Bermuda roads are made by cutting down a few inches into the solid white coral—or a good many feet, where a hill intrudes itself—and smoothing off the surface of the road-bed. It is a simple and easy process. The grain of the coral is coarse and porous; the road-bed has the look of being made of coarse white sugar. Its excessive cleanness and whiteness are a trouble in one way: the sun is reflected into your eyes with such energy as you walk along, that you want to sneeze all the time. . . .

We walked several miles that afternoon in the bewildering glare of the sun, the white roads, and the white buildings. Our eyes got to paining us a good deal. By and by a soothing, blessed twilight spread its cool balm around. We looked up in pleased surprise and saw that it proceeded from an intensely black negro who was going by. We answered his military salute in the grateful gloom of his near presence, and then passed on into the pitiless white glare again.

The colored women whom we met usually bowed and spoke; so did the children. The colored men commonly gave the military salute. They borrow this fashion from the soldiers, no doubt; England has kept a garrison here for generations. The younger men's custom of carrying small canes is also borrowed from the soldiers, I suppose, who always carry a cane, in Bermuda as everywhere else in Britain's broad dominions.

The country roads curve and wind hither and thither in the delightfulest way, unfolding pretty surprises at every turn: billowy masses of oleander that seem to float out from behind distant projections like the pink cloud-banks of sunset; sudden plunges among cottages and gardens, life and activity, followed by as sudden plunges into the sombre twilight and still-ness of the woods; flitting visions of white fortresses and beacon towers pictured against the sky on remote hill-tops; glimpses of shining green sea caught for a moment through opening headlands, then lost again; more woods and solitude; and by and by another turn lays bare, without warning, the full sweep of the inland ocean, enriched with its bars of soft color, and graced with its wandering sails.

Here was an odd manner of travel writing, seemingly topographical but without reference to specific places. Was the inland ocean the Great Sound or Harrington Sound or Castle Harbor? Yet he beautifully captured the meandering, dreamy quality of Bermuda roads, and foretold Howells's description of the Islands as "all atmosphere, an affair of the air and sun and sky."[22] In perceptiveness and style, Mark Twain's words could also surpass innumerable texts by modern city planners:

Take any road you please, you may depend upon it you will not stay in it half a mile. Your road is everything that a road ought to be: it is bordered with trees, and with strange plants and flowers; it is shady and pleasant . . . it carries you by the prettiest and peacefulest and most home-like of homes, and through stretches of forest that lie in a deep hush sometimes, and sometimes are alive with the music of birds; it curves always, which is a continual promise, whereas straight roads reveal everything at a glance and kill interest.

Your road is all this, and yet you will not stay in it half a mile, for the reason that little seductive, mysterious roads are always branching out from it on either hand, and as these curve sharply also and hide what is beyond, you cannot resist the temptation to desert your own chosen road and explore them. You are usually paid for your trouble; consequently, your walk inland always turns out to be one of the most crooked, involved, purposeless, and interesting experiences a body can imagine. There is enough of variety. Sometimes you are in the level open, with marshes thick grown with flag-lances that are ten feet high on the one hand, and potato and onion orchards on the other; next, you are on a hilltop, with the ocean and the Islands spread around you; presently the road winds through a deep cut, shut in by perpendicular walls thirty or forty feet high, marked with the oddest and abruptest stratum lines, suggestive of sudden and eccentric old upheavals, and garnishes with here and there a clinging adventurous flower, and here and there a dangling vine; and by and by your way is along the sea edge, and you may look down a fathom or two through the transparent water and watch the diamond-like flash and play of the light upon the rocks and sands on the bottom until you are tired of it,—if you are so constituted as to be able to get tired of it.

You may march the country roads in maiden meditation, fancy free, by field and farm, for no dog will plunge out at you from unsuspected gate, with breathtaking surprise of ferocious bark, notwithstanding it is a Christian land and a civilized. We saw upwards of a million cats in Bermuda, but the people are very abstemious in the matter of dogs. Two or three nights we prowled the country far and wide, and never once were accosted by a dog. It is a great privilege to visit such a land. The cats were no offense when properly distributed, but when piled they obstructed travel.[23]

After he had drawn from two or three days of touring, and had freely rearranged and combined facts from his notes, Mark Twain reverted to their first evening:

The early twilight of a Sunday evening in Hamilton, Bermuda, is an alluring time. There is just enough of whispering breeze, fragrance of flowers, and sense of repose to raise one's thoughts heavenward; and just enough amateur piano music to keep him reminded of the other place. There are many venerable pianos in Hamilton, and they all play at twilight. Age enlarges and enriches the powers of some musical instruments,— notably those of the violin,—but it seems to set a piano's teeth on edge. Most of the music in vogue there is the same that those pianos prattled in their innocent infancy; and there is something very pathetic about it when they go over it now, in their asthmatic second childhood, dropping a note here and there, where a tooth is gone.

We attended evening service at the stately Episcopal church on the hill, where were five or six hundred people, half of them white and the other half black, according to the usual Bermudian proportions; and all well dressed,—a thing which is also usual in Bermuda and to be confidently expected. There was good music, which we heard, and doubtless a good sermon, but there was a wonderful deal of coughing, and so only the high parts of the argument carried over it. . . .[24]

We went wandering off toward the country, and were soon far down in the lonely black depths of a road that was roofed over with the dense foliage of a double rank of great cedars. There was no sound of any kind, there; it was perfectly still. And it was so dark that one could detect nothing but sombre outlines. We strode farther and farther down this tunnel, cheering the way with chat.

Presently the chat took this shape: "How insensibly the character of a people and of a government makes its impress upon a stranger, and gives him a sense of security or of insecurity without his taking deliberate thought upon the matter or asking anybody a question! We have been in this land half a day; we have seen none but honest faces; we have noted the British flag flying, which means efficient government and good order; so without inquiry we plunge unarmed and with perfect confidence into this dismal place, which in almost any other country would swarm with thugs and garroters—"

'Sh! What was that? Stealthy footsteps! Low voices! We gasp, we close up together, and wait. A vague shape glides out of the dusk and confronts us. A voice speaks—demands money!

"A shilling, gentlemen, if you please, to help build the new Methodist church."

Blessed sound! Holy sound! We contribute with thankful avidity.[25]

They hiked again on Monday morning, and took a carriage ride in the afternoon. Most likely, they took along the *Bermuda Pocket Almanack.* The only palm endemic to the Islands was the palmetto (*Sabal bermudana*), but the little book cited the royal palm (*Roystonea regia*) as one of the curiosities of Bermuda's plant life. The royal palm, also known as the mountain cabbage palm, was native to Cuba. It possessed certain anthropomorphic qualities—a gently swelling torso, graceful neck, and crown of fronds spreading like a full head of hair (FIG. 21). Clemens knew that the value of drawing lay "in training the eye to observe—also to see things as they *are,*" and he made a fine sketch of the tree in his notebook:[26]

During this day and the next we took carriage drives about the island and over to the town of St. George's, fifteen or twenty miles away. Such hard, excellent roads to drive over are not to be found elsewhere out of Europe. An intelligent young colored man drove us, and acted as guidebook. In the edge of the town we saw five or six mountain cabbage palms (atrocious name!) standing in a straight row, and equidistant from each

FIGURE 21. Royal palms, Somers Gardens, town of St. George.

other. These were not the largest or the tallest trees I have ever seen, but they were the stateliest, the most majestic. That row of them must be the nearest that nature has ever come to counterfeiting a colonnade. These trees are all the same height, say sixty feet; the trunks as gray as granite, with a very gradual and perfect taper; without sign of branch or knot or flaw; the surface not looking like bark, but like granite that has been dressed and not polished. Thus all the way up the diminishing shaft for fifty feet; then it begins to take the appearance of being closely wrapped, spool-fashion, with gray cord, or of having been turned in a lathe. Above this point there is an outward swell, and thence upwards, for six feet or more, the cylinder is a bright, fresh green, and is formed of wrappings like those of an ear of green Indian corn. Then comes the great, spraying palm plume, also green. Other palm-trees always lean out of the perpendicular, or have a curve in them. But the plumb-line could not detect a deflection in any individual of this stately row; they stand as straight as the colonnade of Baalbec; they have its great height, they have its gracefulness, they have its dignity; in moonlight or twilight, and shorn of their plumes, they would duplicate it.

The birds we came across in the country were singularly tame; even that wild creature, the quail, would pick around in the grass at ease while we inspected it and talked about it at leisure. A small bird of the canary species had to be stirred up with the butt-end of the whip before it would move, and then it moved only a couple of feet. It is said that even the suspicious flea is tame and sociable in Bermuda, and will allow himself to be caught and caressed without misgivings. . . .

We saw no bugs or reptiles to speak of, and so I was thinking of saying in print, in a general way, that there were none at all; but one night after I had gone to bed, the Reverend came into my room carrying something, and asked, "Is this your boot?" I said it was, and he said he had met a spider going off with it. Next morning he stated that just at dawn the same spider raised his window and was coming in to get a shirt, but saw him and fled.

Howells reported many years later that he, too, encountered spiders "the bigness of bats," and Julia C. R. Dorr, a New England poet who visited the Islands in 1883, said she saw spiders of "exceedingly large proportions."[27] Mark Twain said nothing about the two most noticeable kinds of creatures on the Islands today: the tiny tree frogs, which whistle such delicate serenades, did not arrive until 1880; and the first of three species of Anolis lizards, which can change their colors, was introduced in 1905.[28]

In marveling at the plant life, he forgot to mention the banana trees he had recorded in his notebook:

Here and there on the country roads we found lemon, papaia, orange, lime, and fig trees; also several sorts of palms, among them the cocoa, the date, and the palmetto. We saw some bamboos forty feet high, with stems as thick as a man's arm. Jungles of the mangrove-tree stood up out of swamps, propped on their interlacing roots as upon a tangle of stilts. In dryer places the noble tamarind sent down its grateful cloud of shade. Here and there the blossomy tamarisk adorned the roadside. There was a curious gnarled and twisted black tree, without a single leaf on it. It might have passed itself off for a dead apple-tree but for the fact that it had a star-like red-hot flower sprinkled sparsely over its person. It had the scattery red glow that a constellation might have when glimpsed through smoked glass. . . .

We saw a tree that bears grapes, and just as calmly and unostentatiously as a vine would do it. We saw an India-rubber tree, but out of season, possibly, so there were no shoes on it, nor suspenders, nor anything that a person would properly expect to find there. This gave it an impressively fraudulent look. There was exactly one mahogany-tree on the island. I know this to be reliable, because I saw a man who said he had counted it many a time and could not be mistaken. He was a man with a hare lip and a pure heart, and everybody said he was as true as steel. Such men are all too few.

The *Pocket Almanack* also cited the handsome mahogany tree (*Swietenia mahogani*), then some twenty years old, at the meeting of the Harrington Sound Road and the Middle Road, in Flatts Village. The tree still thrives (FIG. 22). It was mentioned in later guidebooks, and also identified on the *Tourist's Map of the Bermuda Islands* published by James H. Stark in 1890. Samuel Musson planted the splendid tree at the gate to Palmetto Grove, his home, and in his old age liked to rest in its shade. (Other mahogany trees, none so old or colossal, now grow on the Islands.)[29] Mark Twain continued:

One's eye caught near and far the pink cloud of the oleander and the red blaze of the pomegranate blossom. In one piece of wild wood the morning-glory vines had wrapped the trees to their very tops, and decorated them all over with couples and clusters of great blue bells,—a fine and striking spectacle, at a little distance. But the dull cedar is everywhere,

FIGURE 22. Mahogany tree, Flatts Village.

and its is the prevailing foliage. One does not appreciate how dull it is until the varnished, bright green attire of the infrequent lemon-tree pleasantly intrudes its contrast. In one thing Bermuda is eminently tropical,—was in May, at least,—the unbrilliant, slightly faded, unrejoicing look of the landscape. For forests arrayed in a blemishless magnificence of glowing green foliage that seems to exult in its own existence and can move the beholder to an enthusiasm that will make him either shout or cry, one must go to countries that have malignant winters.

He had written in his notebook that from the prevalence of the cedar (*Juniperus bermudiana*), "you almost get the impression that it is the *only* tree here." Trollope, too, complained that Bermuda was almost entirely covered with "small stunted bushy cedar trees," and Howells spoke of the "scraggy foliage" of the Bermuda cedar.[30] (An epidemic of scale insects in the 1940s transformed the landscape. Spreading from infested trees imported from California, the insects killed about 95 percent of the endemic cedars.)

Mark Twain, again:

> We saw scores of colored farmers digging their crops of potatoes and onions, their wives and children helping,—entirely contented and comfortable, if looks go for anything. We never met a man, or woman, or child anywhere in this sunny island who seemed to be unprosperous, or discontented, or sorry about anything. This sort of monotony became very tiresome presently, and even something worse. The spectacle of an entire nation grovelling in contentment is an infuriating thing. We felt the lack of something in this community,—a vague, an undefinable, an elusive something, and yet a lack. But after considerable thought we made out what it was,—tramps. Let them go there, right now, in a body. It is utterly virgin soil. Passage is cheap. Every true patriot in America will help buy tickets. Whole armies of these excellent beings can be spared from our midst and our polls; they will find a delicious climate and a green, kind-hearted people. There are potatoes and onions for all, and a generous welcome for the first batch that arrives, and elegant graves for the second. . . .
>
> The island is not large. Somewhere in the interior a man ahead of us had a very slow horse. I suggested that we had better go by him; but the driver said the man had but a little way to go. I waited to see, wondering how he could know. Presently the man did turn down another road. I asked, "How did you know he would?"
>
> "Because I knew the man, and where he lived."
>
> I asked him, satirically, if he knew everybody in the island; he answered, very simply, that he did. This gives a body's mind a good substantial grip on the dimensions of the place.

Bermuda perhaps lacked tramps, but there must have been signs of the unprosperous (FIG. 23). Clemens and Twichell crossed the Causeway and arrived that day, Tuesday, in St. George. They repaired to the Globe Hotel at 32 Duke of York Street (FIG. 24). A ponderous stone structure with huge chimneys, the Globe was built in 1699–1700 as a house for the governor. In the Civil War years

FIGURE 23. "Pity the Blind," about 1910.

it sheltered the agent of the Confederacy. The hotel registry for May 22, 1877, bears the signatures "S. Langhorne" and "J. H. Twichell USA."

Mark Twain's account:

At the principal hotel in St. George's, a young girl, with a sweet, serious face, said we could not be furnished with dinner, because we had not been expected, and no preparation had been made. . . . I said we were not very hungry; a fish would do. My little maid answered, it was not the market-day for fish. Things began to look serious; but presently the boarder who sustained the hotel came in, and when the case was laid before him he was cheerfully willing to divide. So we had much pleasant chat at table about St. George's chief industry, the repairing of damaged ships; and in between we had a soup that had something in it that seemed to taste like the hereafter, but it proved to be only pepper of a particularly vivacious kind. And we had an iron-clad chicken that was

FIGURE 24. Globe Hotel, town of St. George.

FIGURE 25. Board-and-batten shutter, town of St. George.

deliciously cooked, but not in the right way. Baking was not the thing to convince his sort. . . . No matter; we had potatoes and a pie and a sociable good time. Then a ramble through the town, which is a quaint one, with interesting, crooked streets, and narrow, crooked lanes, with here and there a grain of dust. Here, as in Hamilton, the dwellings had Venetian blinds of a very sensible pattern. They were not double shutters, hinged at the sides, but a single broad shutter, hinged at the top; you push it outward, from the bottom, and fasten it at any angle required by the sun or desired by yourself.

Elsewhere, he wrote of the haunting sounds from shutters rattling in the wind, and told of shutters that served as ready litters for the sick and wounded. But in St. George he paid no attention to the full range of shutter types, or their great power of poetic expression. Top-hinged shutters, known on the Islands as pushout blinds, were propped open with notched sticks or oversized metal hooks and eyes (see FIG. 8). Side-hinged shutters, louvered or of solid wood in board-and-batten (plainly, the primitive type) or paneling, were also put to use (FIG. 25). All kinds of shutters—nicely defined by Joseph Gwilt, the nineteenth-century encyclopedist, as "the doors of window openings"—performed as sunshades. They also protected the caulking of windowpanes from drying and cracking; guarded a house against high winds, rain, and debris hurled by storms; forestalled burglars; and all the while maintained ventilation and privacy. Shutters brought life to inert masonry walls and eased transitions from walls to openings. From their presence, moreover, subtle modulations of interior light could evoke mystery and romance.[31]

Mark Twain turned next to the large catchments for rainwater:

All about the island one sees great white scars on the hill-slopes. These are dished spaces where the soil has been scraped off and the coral exposed and glazed with hard whitewash. Some of these are a quarter-acre in size. They catch and carry the rainfall to reservoirs; for the wells are few and poor, and there are no natural springs and no brooks.

They say that the Bermuda climate in mild and equable, with never any snow or ice, and that one may be very comfortable in spring clothing the year round, there. We had delightful and decided summer weather in May, with a flaming sun that permitted the thinnest of raiment, and yet there was a constant breeze; consequently we were never discomforted by heat. At four or five in the afternoon the mercury began to go down, and then it became necessary to change to thick garments. I went to St. George's in the morning clothed in the thinnest of linen, and reached home at five in the afternoon with two overcoats on. The nights are said to be always cool and bracing. We had mosquito nets, and the Reverend said the mosquitoes persecuted him a good deal. I often heard him slapping and banging at these imaginary creatures with as much zeal as if they had been real. There are no mosquitoes in the Bermudas in May.

The poet Thomas Moore spent several months in Bermuda more than seventy years ago. He was sent out to be registrar of the admiralty. I am not quite clear as to the function of a registrar of the admiralty of Bermuda, but I think it is his duty to keep a record of all the admirals born there.

Moore owed his brief sinecure in Bermuda to his patron, the Earl of Moira. The poet lived in St. George. (The house called "Tom Moore's Tavern," by Castle Harbor, is Walsingham House. The most historic dwelling in Hamilton Parish, it dates from late in the seventeenth century. Moore was merely a guest there of Samuel Trott's.) On his arrival in January 1804, Moore became registrar to the Court of Vice Admiralty, charged with recording data about captured ships for adjudication. Quickly bored, he left the Islands in April. Bermudian women, he wrote, "though not generally handsome, have an affectionate languor in their look and manner, which is always interesting." He considered the men not very civilized.[32]

Rainy weather on Wednesday dissuaded Clemens and Twichell from a sailboat outing. The next day, May 24, was Empire Day, a holiday in celebration of Queen Victoria's birthday. It rained again. At one o'clock that morning a grandchild was born to Mrs. Kirkham, and by four o'clock in the afternoon Clemens and Twichell were back at sea, on their way to New York. Clemens made more notebook entries on shipboard. "Bermuda is free (at present) from the triple curse of railways, telegraphs & newspapers," he wrote, "but this will not outlast next year. I propose to spend next year there & no more."[33]

He revised those thoughts for the "Idle Excursion":

There are several "sights" in the Bermudas, of course, but they are easily avoided. This is a great advantage,—one cannot have it in Europe.

Bermuda is the right country for a jaded man to "loaf" in. There are no harassments; the deep peace and quiet of the country sink into one's body and bones and give his conscience a rest, and chloroform the legion of invisible small devils that are always trying to whitewash his hair. . . .

The Bermudians are hoping soon to have telegraphic communication with the world. But even after they shall have acquired this curse it will still be a good country to go to for a vacation, for there are charming little islets scattered about the enclosed sea where one could live secure from interruption. The telegraph boy would have to come in a boat, and one could easily kill him while he was making his landing.

III

Hints from the Notebook

Clemens had invited William Dean Howells to Bermuda, but he declined. "I suppose you're going to sea for your health," Howells wrote on May 15. "You're an enviable man to be able to go. I know *one* set of shaky nerves that can't." Days with Clemens were exhilarating, Howells knew, but exhausting. ("Your visit was a perfect ovation for us: we *never* enjoy anything so much as those visits of yours," he had written Clemens a few months earlier. "The smoke and the Scotch and the late hours almost kill us; but we look each other in the eyes when [you] are gone, and say what a glorious time it was.")[1] Howells sailed to Bermuda in later years, but never with Clemens. In a letter of May 29, Clemens chided:

> Confound you, Joe Twichell & I roamed about Bermuda day & night & never ceased to gabble & enjoy—About half the talk was—"It is a burning shame that Howells isn't here." . . .
>
> O, your insufferable pride, which will have a fall some day! If you had gone with us & let me pay the $50 which the trip, & the board & the various nick-nacks & mementoes would cost, I would have picked up enough droppings from your conversation to pay me 500 per cent profit in the way of the *several* magazine articles which I could have written, whereas I can now write only one or two & am therefore largely out of

pocket by your proud ways. Ponder these things. Lord, what a perfectly bewitching excursion it was! I traveled under an assumed name & was never molested with a polite attention from *any*body.

Once he got home, Twichell wrote in his journal that he and Clemens enjoyed "a very pleasant time" and drove around the Islands, "which we inspected pretty thoroughly."[2] In light of the reverend's matter-of-fact and pedestrian style, the report in the *Hartford Courant* must have been informed primarily by Clemens:

> They went out on the regular steamer which sailed from New York a week ago last Thursday, and came back by the same boat. . . . This gave them four days for the sights of the snug little British island; and as it needs only three days to exhaust its attractions, they had a day to spare. They report the onion crop fully up to the average. Bermuda is proud of three things—its onions, its potatoes, and its roads. It is a delightful island to walk over; and if one is fond of onions, there is no place in the world where his taste can be so perfectly gratified. . . . The travelers found the weather in Bermuda charming, and linen suits the comfortable wear.[3]

Clemens immediately set to work on his articles for the *Atlantic*. He was halfway through when he left Hartford on June 6 to spend the summer in Elmira, New York. "I have written two Numbers of my 'Random Notes of an Idle Excursion' (you see that does not indicate whither the ship is bound & therefore the reader can't be saying 'Why all this introduction—are we never coming to Bermuda?')," he wrote Howells that day. "It begins to look as if this Excursion may string out to 4 or 6 Numbers." By June 27 he had "completed the trip" in only four articles, but he harbored such doubts about the first two pieces that he told Howells they could be thrown out. Howells did not agree. In phrasing the title, Clemens exhibited his typical quirkiness. How idle could the excursion have been if it generated so much writing? Nor did the articles relate very closely to his notebook. And of course it was redundant to describe his style as rambling. For years, he had cultivated a slow, disjointed way of telling humorous stories. Moreover, having seen both his father and his brother Orion in perpetual struggle to sustain a precarious living, he wrote to make money; he inflated his books to a hefty size for better sales by subscription, and sometimes distended his magazine pieces because he got paid by the word. Thus a major paradox. He prized clean and condensed prose constructed from an exact and happy choice of words, but, as Mark Twain, deliberately produced long digressions, heavy-handed sarcasms, burlesques, and parodies carried to the point of exhaustion.[4]

Hence his Bermuda idyll became cluttered with macabre tales of no relation to the subject. He republished one separately as "The Captain's Story." Another was so tasteless that Howells excised it. Clemens later revived the tale ("The Invalid's Story"), and published it in three different collections of his sketches. Some stories expressed obliquely the slower days at sea, when, as he jotted in his notebook, "a man eats like an animal & sleeps a dead dreamless stupor half the day & all the night." More basically, they reflected the constant presence of death in nineteenth-century life. In one of Mark Twain's chapters in *The Gilded Age* a child memorably exclaims that "if you stay here you'll see lots of funerals"; and when he published an article many years later on "How to Tell a Story," both of his examples involved corpses.[5] Clemens saw too much of death. Three of his five siblings died before he reached his twenty-third birthday, and eventually he outlived not only his wife, Livy, but three of their four children. Reasonably enough, he held life to be as fragile, evanescent, and soon-to-be-forgotten as a soap bubble. But even at the beginning of his career, and despite his wonderful humor, Mark Twain wrote of impostors, frauds, and swindlers and peopled his stories with skeletons and ghosts, corpses and their coffins.[6]

The articles on Bermuda also displayed his strangely relaxed manner of conflating fact and fiction. He said in the preface to *Roughing It* that he wanted to write from having been "on the ground in person." And he possessed all that was needed to be a first-rate journalist: keen powers of observation, a robust skepticism, a good memory, a vast range of interests, the desire to understand the how and why of things, the ability to talk easily with persons from all walks of life, and the skill to write vivid, compact, precise, and splendidly descriptive prose. But he knew that what passed for a newspaper story was merely a report, superficially informative and almost never well written. Straight reporting—the "unimaginative devotion to petrified facts"—lacked the structure, rhythm, and surprise of true storytelling.[7] The best stories, he asserted, need not be literally factual. Veteran staff members of the *San Francisco Morning Call* told the young Rudyard Kipling that Mark Twain had been incapable of reporting according to the needs of the day, that what he wrote infuriated the editor, but had readers asking for more. After he crossed the country, Kipling was thrilled to meet his idol. "*I* have seen Mark Twain this golden morning," he wrote, "have shaken his hand, and smoked a cigar—no, two cigars—with him, and talked with him for more than two hours!" Kipling listened to him say, "Get your facts first, and then you can distort 'em as much as you please."[8]

In writing the "Idle Excursion," Mark Twain pretended he had never seen Bermuda, but any reader of *The Innocents Abroad* knew better. It could have been true that by traveling as S. Langhorne he escaped much notice by the general public. Five days after he sailed from the Islands, the *Royal Gazette* reported that "'Mark Twain,' the very amusing author, has again visited Bermuda, but on this occasion he concealed his *nom de plume* and none of his former acquaintances here recognized him." But the entries in his notebook revealed that his presence on the Islands did not pass unknown. Abbreviated and occasionally cryptic, his notes were like the diagrams he made for seemingly impromptu lectures that in fact he painstakingly rehearsed. Various motifs in the notebook did not find their way into the *Atlantic Monthly* series. Conversely, his articles contained matter not reflected in the notes. Sometimes he purported to quote from notes that did not truly exist, or his notes contradicted what he wrote. He slighted the usual tourist sights in the "Idle Excursion," but his notebook showed that he visited Devil's Hole, the oldest attraction on the Islands (FIG. 26). "Devil's Hole," his note read, "angel fish, blue & yellow." The collapsed sea cavern, also known as Neptune's Grotto or Groupers' Grotto, had been a commercial operation since the 1830s. Situated by Harrington Sound, in Smith's Parish, it was fed instead by a narrow passage to the ocean. The *Royal Gazette* described Devil's Hole as "an enchanting walled fish-pond," and the *Bermuda Pocket Almanack* promised that "you will see a few of the beautiful Angelfish . . . gliding timidly between the great unsightly groupers." Lady Brassey said the groupers were "fierce, voracious creatures," and Julia Dorr wrote of their "great sluggish bodies and horribly human faces." *Harper's Monthly* reported in 1874 that Devil's Hole was usually stocked with one thousand fish, "though it will hold twice as many."[9] By 1883, the *New York Times* correspondent could see only fourteen groupers, one angelfish, two turtles, and a solitary fish he could not identify. A few years later, Howells found many more:

> In this deep pool, sunken in the rock, live several hundred groupers, a fish with no more distinction than a cod, crowded together, and apparently always hungry. They have big heads and enormous mouths, which are blood-red inside, and when they are packed together, standing on

FIGURE 26. Devil's Hole.

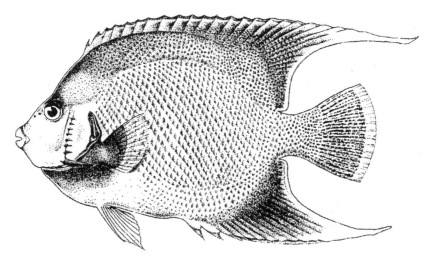

FIGURE 27. Bermuda angelfish (drawn by Christiane Schoepfer-Sterrer, courtesy Wolfgang E. Sterrer).

their tails, with open mouths lifted out of the water in expectation of the bread which is thrown to them, they present in their ravenous obtrusiveness as disgusting a sight as can anywhere be seen. We had an impression that this must be the Washington of the islands, where all the politicians were standing on their tails with their mouths wide open. This is enough to say about the groupers.[10]

Howells, too, was impressed by the beauty of the Bermuda angelfish (*Holacanthus bermudensis*), which he accurately described as "flat and oval in form, of a cerulean blue, with two long streamers edged with yellow." He pronounced it "apparently one of the happiest, as he is one of the most graceful, of all marine inhabitants" (FIG. 27).[11] Clemens, however, saw the angelfish as female. An obscure notebook entry—"The Admiral's secretary & the angel fish"—defies explication, but in later years he made friends with schoolgirls and referred to them as the angelfish of his aquarium.

Clemens also made notes about the impressive homes of the U.S. consul and his deputy, which stand at opposite sides of Flatts Village. Neither is mentioned in the "Idle Excursion." Human nature always remembers contact with the illustrious, he had written in *The Innocents Abroad;* but as Mark Twain, he said later, he "hunted for bigger game—the masses." To boast an easy familiarity with high officials or the privileged could alienate readers. He wrote in his autobiography that times with the uncelebrated ought to be considered just as interesting, and of course they were vastly more numerous. Although he expressed an equal regard for all, Clemens acknowledged the advantages of an aristocracy, and revered the years when steamboat pilots on the Mississippi were men of imposing grandeur, "the envied aristocrats of the river towns."[12]

Flatts Village arose at the crossroads between Smith's Parish and Hamilton Parish, and in the twentieth century would become the site of the public Aquarium, Natural History Museum, and Zoo, an institution that easily eclipsed Devil's Hole. Flatts embraced a picturesque inlet through which the ocean fed Harrington Sound, a large saltwater lagoon (FIGS. 28 AND 29). Water rushes in or out beneath the Flatts bridge at every change of tide. The mahogany tree encountered on the way to Devil's Hole flourished not far from what Clemens's notebook identified as the "Palatial front fence of Vice Consul." This was a long and well-articulated stone wall that still guards the Villa Mont Clare, at 10 Harrington Sound Road (FIG. 30). William Whitney, known as a member of the family prominent in New York, became vice-consul in 1872. Three years later he

FIGURE 28. Flatts inlet.

FIGURE 29. Harrington Sound and Holy Trinity Church, Hamilton Parish.

married Frances Mary Hill, a wealthy Bermudian whose family properties in-
cluded both Mont Clare and the house next door, Villa Monticello. (The *New
York Times* correspondent was a guest of Whitney's in 1883, and wrote of the
"snow-white villas" next to each other. He rated Mont Clare one of the two
finest residences on the Islands, "a gem of a place—pure white in a nest of green,
the heavy white wall that surrounds the grounds peeping out from beneath
vines and flowers.")[13]

Clemens left no record of whether Whitney entertained him, or he simply
paused to admire the stone wall, but when he returned to Flatts in the spring of
1908 he was photographed at Mont Clare. He also knew the home of Charles
M. Allen, the American consul so abused during the Civil War. "Bewitching
place on a lovely inlet where the consul lives," Clemens wrote. This was Wistowe, a severely Georgian house ornamented with an Ionic portico (FIG. 31).
Sited on the North Shore Road, at the west edge of the village, Wistowe had
been built long before Allen's time. The consul improved the house consider-
ably, the *Bermuda Pocket Almanack* reported, and embellished the garden front
with a fountain powered by the tide through an old canal. Julia Dorr, when she
wrote of voyaging to Bermuda in the spring of 1883, said she visited "the quaint
and beautiful home of the American consul," and saw in the fountain basin
"dozens of beautiful angelfish."[14]

In the most intriguing of his notes, Clemens said that just as he and Twichell
were about to leave the Islands, "Mr. Allen, the American consul, came aboard
to inquire after Charly [sic] Langdon & mother." So much for his pretense of
having traveled incognito.[15] Throughout the notebook, almost obsessively,
Clemens complained about occasional noises, out-of-tune pianos, and their
out-of-date melodies. He wrote on the first morning that "the calm Sabbath is
being profaned by the crowing & clucking of chickens, the wauling of cats &
the clanging of a metallic neighboring piano." A piano disturbed him again on
Monday morning by sounding the same notes. "That same old tune," he wrote
on Tuesday morning, "& that same rooster." Later that day, in St. George: "Globe
Hotel piano same aged pattern. Must have been a musical epidemic here some
30 years ago, which died early. The pianos & songs are all of that date." And on
Wednesday: "That piano & that tune & that rooster were silent this morning."
The state of pianos on the Islands could be surmised from an advertisement in
the *Royal Gazette* that offered a sweet-toned instrument with a metal frame and
French action "extra bolted for the climate." Thomas Moore had written his
mother about the bothersome pianofortes. Precisely because the Islands were so

FIGURE 30. Villa Mont Clare, Smith's Parish.

FIGURE 31. Wistowe, Hamilton Parish.

quiet, any music or noise carried far, and interrupted the silence and solitude so dear to writers. "All sane people detest noise," Mark Twain wrote later. "Only about two men in a hundred can play upon a musical instrument, and not four in a hundred have any wish to learn how."[16]

Clemens recorded in his notebook that a few "wretched" wood houses in St. George stood at the edge of town in "villainous contrast to the tidy coral ones." (A small wood house east of town on Cut Road was destroyed by Hurricane Fabian on September 5, 2003.) He also wrote that the parishes of Bermuda "are jealous of & blackguard each other—playfully & otherwise." Mistakenly, he thought there were eight parishes, rather than nine: an error perhaps due to the fact that the Islands were divided originally into eight "tribes" or small parishes, with the common or "Generall land," as early maps spelled it, reserved at the East End. (The common land became St. George's Parish, the other parishes being Hamilton, Smith's, Devonshire, Paget, Pembroke, Warwick, Southampton, and Sandys—all names that should have discouraged anyone from thinking the settlers were Spanish.)

The voyage to Bermuda in the spring of 1877 greatly satisfied Clemens, just as the "Idle Excursion" pleased Howells at the *Atlantic*. "I've just been reading aloud to my wife your Bermuda papers," Howells wrote on June 30. "That they're delightfully entertaining goes without saying; but we also found that you gave us the only realizing sense of Bermuda that we've ever had."[17] Clemens had already written Twichell. "It was much the joyousest trip I ever had, Joe—not a heartache in it," he said, "not a twinge of conscience."

IV

THIRTY YEARS LATER, 1907

Mark Twain's fame inevitably benefited Bermuda, and the Islands gained further attention in 1883, when Princess Louise of Canada arrived for a winter respite. She was a daughter of Queen Victoria, and was grandly hailed as "the first real live Princess who ever gladdened Bermuda with her presence."[1] The appearance of a royal personage in a place so isolated as Bermuda spurred even the *New York Times* to dispatch a special correspondent, unnamed, who feebly tried to imitate Mark Twain's style. People kept repeating Mark Twain's harmless jokes about the Indian rubber tree, he reported, and lavished attention on Mrs. Kirkham's Private Boarding House. "They point out here with pride the house Mark Twain lived in while he was in Bermuda," he said, "and it is nothing extra of a house either."[2] Princess Louise had sailed on the *Dido,* a British warship. She reached Her Majesty's Dockyard on January 29. James H. Trimingham, the founder of a notable dry goods house, graciously lent her his fine two-story home called Inglewood, newly built on a large estate in Paget Parish. "The mansion with its spacious rooms and rich draperies is fit for any princess," a citizen wrote in the *Royal Gazette,* which admitted that neither Government House nor Admiralty House qualified.[3] Princess Louise must have heard talk about Mark Twain. She stayed until April 10, and the next month she and her husband, the Marquis of Lorne, governor-general of Canada, entertained Clemens in Ottawa.

A new hotel named the Princess opened in Hamilton at the end of 1884. Bermuda was preparing for a larger number of tourists, most of them from the eastern seaboard. By 1890 the Islands were known as a haven for well-to-do Americans. "Bermuda is by no means a disagreeable spot," the *Graphic* said that year, "and the climate is very pleasant." William Dean Howells wrote in 1894 that Bermuda appealed especially to the Yankee with money and leisure. "By so short a voyage in no other direction can he get so completely out of the world," Howells said, "or be so protected from the disturbances of modern life." Such peacefulness arose primarily from the absence of American newspapers, he said. The mail from the States came only once a week, and the "so-called news" by way of Halifax was much delayed. Howells returned in 1901, and described Bermuda as a place "where time is so long that if you lose your patience you easily find it again." Much like Clemens, he considered Bermuda a paradise—one that had an advantage over Eden. Apparently, it was not woman and her seed who were expelled, he wrote, but the serpent and *his* seed, for "women now abound in the Summer Islands, and there is not a snake anywhere to be found."[4]

By the turn of the century, Mark Twain had published all of his best-known books. His life had been hectic, and exceedingly peripatetic; a bare outline now commands pages and pages. He reached "Pier No. 70" on November 30, 1905, and was soon celebrated at Delmonico's, in New York, with a banquet staged by George Harvey, who edited both *Harper's Weekly* and the *North American Review.* Clemens said he attained the scriptural statute of limitations "by sticking strictly to a scheme of life which would kill anybody else." Death had taken instead his little son Langdon, his favored daughter Susy, and his wife, Livy. After business ventures as ill-advised as betting on the jumping frog, he paid his creditors in full and was back in the money. He was leasing a house at 21 Fifth Avenue, at Ninth Street. The next year, Clemens said that by forty years of slavery to the pen he had earned his freedom. "If I haven't done my share of work," he wrote later, "I have at least reached the time limit when I ought to have done it."[5] He had made Mark Twain a great name on the world's stage, an instantly recognized character pleased to be captured in thousands of photographs. But the concerns of the world no longer held much interest for him, he admitted in a speech at the Waldorf-Astoria. "Now, you see before you the wreck and ruin of what was once a young person like yourselves," he said. "I am exhausted by the heat of the day. I must take what is left of this wreck and ruin out of your presence and carry it away to my home and spread it out there and sleep the sleep of the righteous. There is nothing much left of me but my age and my righteousness."[6]

Clemens had not set foot for many years in either Hawaii or Bermuda, his favorite island places. In the fall of 1906 he talked about a journey to Egypt, then abandoned the idea after another siege of bronchitis. He was renting a summer house in Dublin, New Hampshire. To cheer himself for presenting a lecture one cold October night, he wore a white suit. "I made a brave experiment," he said in dictating his autobiography, "to see how it would feel to shock a crowd with these unseasonable clothes. . . . Little by little I hope to get together courage enough to wear white clothes all through the winter, in New York. It will be a great satisfaction to me to show off in this way." Howells, who must have forgotten the sealskin coat and sealskin cap, said that before Clemens took to wearing white suits in winter he had been "aggressively indifferent about dress." The grand moment came on December 7, and not in New York but in Washington, D.C., where Clemens appeared in ghostly white to testify before a congressional committee on copyright. He gained all the attention he craved.[7]

The same month, though, he suffered from both bronchitis and gout. The warm, pleasant climate of Bermuda came to mind, and he invited George Harvey to join him in sailing to the Islands. Colonel Harvey was an exceedingly busy man, and Clemens did well enough to catch him for a few games of billiards. A weeklong holiday was too much to ask. Clemens thought next of his kindly old friend Twichell. In the years since their idle excursion of 1877, the reverend had voyaged twice more to Bermuda. Clemens asked his secretary, Isabel V. Lyon, to invite Twichell. She, too, had been to the Islands, some eighteen years earlier, and was eager to go again. An intelligent and determined woman, Miss Lyon joined the Clemens family late in 1902 at the house they were renting in Riverdale, New York, to serve as Livy's secretary. She very soon began to assist Clemens as well, then took over the management of the entire household, wherever it should happen to be. Her adoration of Clemens knew no bounds. "All my days are hallowed by Mr. Clemens's wonderful presence," she wrote in her daybook for December 14, 1906, and on the following May 30 she characterized him as "the most wonderful creature in the world."[8]

Amid the long series of toasts to Clemens at his seventieth birthday party, Howells called him "the King," and so did George Washington Cable, the southern novelist who so many years earlier teamed with Mark Twain on the speaking platform. Miss Lyon was happy to follow suit. "The King is planning to go to Bermuda if Mr. Twichell can go too," she noted late in December 1906. "Mr. Clemens would like to go there for the sun. . . . He thinks he'd like the isolation, but the lack of companionship would make more desolation for him than anything else, for he of all people must have companionship—mental companion-ship." Twichell's acceptance came the day after Christmas. They could bunk to-gether if necessary, Clemens remarked, but "in matters of theology we differ" and it would be better to put Twichell in the forecastle. At year's end, the *New York Herald* published a guide to winter resorts. The beauties of Bermuda, the paper said, were immortalized by the poet Tom Moore, and Mark Twain—"as much poet as humorist"—had added his tribute:

> And now the Bermuda season is already in full swing. The Quebec steamship line already has so large a booking that it may be compelled to put another steamer in this particular service during the height of the season. The big, roomy twin screw steamer *Bermudian,* which was built specially to meet the demands of increased travel and placed on the line two seasons ago, accommodates 238 first class passengers. . . .
>
> Bermuda has developed into an all year resort. . . . Last summer from 1,500 to 2,000 excursionists visited the place, an increase of forty per cent over last year. Five years ago no one visited the resort during the summer months. . . .
>
> A stranger floating over the white shoals of a coral reef for the first time will be wonderstruck by the marvellous clearness of the sea water and the strange effect of deception as to depth. Objects which appear to reach nearly to the surface are found to be so deep that the vessel passes safely over them. The sunlight reaches many fathoms down. . . . And the color—that beautiful bewildering green, just the shade that one catches in the gleam of an opal or the tint of a malachite. Painters have sought in vain to rival it with their pigments.[9]

Clemens, Twichell, and Miss Lyon sailed on Wednesday, January 2 (FIG. 32). The trip now took two days rather than three. "People are not disturbing the King," Miss Lyon wrote on Thursday. "The one woman who tried to, I told that the King wished to be let alone, *must* be let alone, because he had come away ex-hausted." Twichell presented a different annoyance. He was losing his hearing, she said, and the King nearly lost his patience. The *Bermudian* made land at six o'clock on Friday morning, and approached Hamilton Harbor through Two Rock Passage, a newer and better channel than Timlins' Narrows (FIG. 33). It docked about nine thirty (FIG. 34). The white houses inspired Miss Lyon to wax

FIGURE 32. Clemens with Miss Lyon and Reverend Twichell on the RMS *Bermudian,* 1907 (courtesy the Mark Twain Project, the Bancroft Library).

FIGURE 33. The Great Sound, looking south toward Two Rock Passage.

FIGURE 34. Hamilton Harbor, 1899, looking northeast (Coit album, courtesy the Bermuda Archives).

poetic; they had grown a thousand years ago as if plants, she wrote, and "somehow you do not feel the hand of man, because there isn't anything inappropriate about them." Clemens and his party registered at the Princess Hotel, which stood by the water not far west of town (FIG. 35). It was the largest wood building on the Islands, and its structure had been advertised as "a sure *guarantee* against the dampness usually found in houses."[10] The dining hall opened through glass doors to a long and deep veranda overlooking the harbor. Another amenity, the billiard room on the ground floor, also came close to Clemens's heart. He had been spending an immoderate amount of time at billiards. As he grew lonelier, the games got longer. They sometimes lasted for as much as ten hours, Miss Lyon wrote.

Friday afternoon they all took a long carriage drive to Harrington Sound. "We went into the Devil's Cave [*sic*]," Miss Lyon said, "where the King was interested in the great big groupers and beautiful angel fish, and butterfly fish and parrot fish. . . . But most of all, I am in heaven as I sat beside the King and drove along those beautiful roads." On Saturday morning they chartered a boat named the *Nautilus,* and sailed in and out of the bays and inlets for two and a half hours. "The King smoked and smoked," she wrote, "and talked about Marconi

FIGURE 35. The Princess Hotel, about 1900 (courtesy the Bermuda Archives).

and Tesla and Joe Jefferson and of how 40 years ago out in Nevada when he had prospected for gold and didn't get it after all their hard work, it was because they had turned in the wrong direction." After lunch, she and Clemens visited the Royal Bermuda Yacht Club, then on Front Street near the docks. Clemens left his visiting card. He no longer pretended to be traveling incognito, and had just been interviewed by the *Colonist,* a paper that once competed with the *Royal Gazette* but now has been lost from memory. Clemens and Miss Lyon took a drive past Government House, by the North Shore. "He is so gentle and gay when Mr. Twichell doesn't make him too nervous," she wrote.

Sunday, their last full day on the Islands, they spent riding through Paget and Warwick, then back northeast to Hamilton Parish and to Joyce's Dock Caves, close to the Causeway. The caves that year were advertised in the *Bermuda Pocket Almanack* as the finest sight in Bermuda, being "brilliantly lit with acetylene gas, showing stalactites of enormous size." (In more recent years, the principal cave has been known as Prospero's Cave, once a nightclub and now merely on the premises of the Grotto Bay Beach Resort.) After they returned to town, Clemens set out to recover something of his visit in 1877, when he and Twichell enjoyed a boardinghouse freedom. The interlude immediately became part of his ongoing autobiography:

⌇ Sometimes a thought, by the power of association, will bring back to your mind a lost word or a lost name which you have not been able to recover by any other process known to your mental equipment. Yesterday we had an instance of this.

Rev. Joseph H. Twichell is with me on this flying trip to Bermuda. He was with me on my last visit to Bermuda, and to-day we were trying to remember when it was; we thought it was somewhere in the neighborhood of thirty years ago, but that was as near as we could get at the date. Twichell said that the landlady in whose boarding-house we sojourned in that ancient time could doubtless furnish us the date, and we must look her up. We wanted to see her, anyway, because she and her blooming daughter of eighteen were the only persons whose acquaintance we had made at that time, for we were traveling under fictitious names, and people who wear aliases are not given to seeking society and bringing themselves under suspicion. But at this point in our talk we encountered an obstruction; we could not recall the landlady's name. . . . We finally gave the matter up, and fell to talking about something else. The talk wandered from one subject to another, and finally arrived at Twichell's school days in Hartford—the Hartford of something more than half a century ago—and he mentioned several of his schoolmasters, dwelling with special interest upon the peculiarities of an aged one named Olney. He remarked that Olney, humble village schoolmaster as he was, was yet a man of superior parts, and had published text-books which had enjoyed a wide currency in America in their day. I said I remembered those books, and had studied Olney's Geography in school when I was a boy. Then Twichell said,

"That reminds me—our landlady's name was a name that was associated with school-books of some kind or other, fifty or sixty years ago. I wonder what it was. I believe it began with K."

Association did the rest, and did it instantly. I said, "Kirkham's Grammar!"

That settled it. Kirkham was the name; and we went out to seek for the owner of it. There was no trouble about that, for Bermuda is not large, and is like the earlier Garden of Eden, in that everybody in it knows everybody else, just as it was in the serpent's headquarters in Adam's time. We easily found Miss Kirkham—she that had been the blooming girl of a generation before—and she was still keeping boarders; but her mother had passed from this life. She settled the date for us, and did it with certainty, by help of a couple of uncommon circumstances, events of that ancient time. She said we had sailed from Bermuda on the 24th of May, 1877, which was the day on which her only nephew was born—and he is now thirty years of age. The other unusual circumstance—she called it an unusual circumstance, and I didn't say anything—was that on that day the Rev. Mr. Twichell (bearing the assumed name of Peters) had made a statement to her which she regarded as a fiction. I remembered the circumstance very well. We had bidden the young girl good-bye and had gone fifty yards, perhaps, when Twichell said he had forgotten something (I doubted it) and must go back. When he rejoined me he was silent, and this alarmed me, because I had not seen an example of it before. He seemed quite uncomfortable, and I asked him what the trouble was. He said he had been inspired to give the girl a pleasant surprise, and so had gone back and said to her—

"That young fellow's name is not Wilkinson—that's Mark Twain."

She did not lose her mind; she did not exhibit any excitement at all, but said quite simply, quite tranquilly,

"Tell it to the marines, Mr. Peters—if that should happen to be *your* name."

It was very pleasant to meet her again. We were white-headed, but she was not; in the sweet and unvexed spiritual atmosphere of the Bermudas one does not achieve gray hairs at forty-eight.[11]

The story was a bit fuzzy in relation to fact. Twichell used his own name, and Clemens traveled as S. Langhorne. "Wilkinson" was a fictive character in *The Innocents Abroad* meant to illustrate the crudeness of American tourists, the "pitiful nobodies" who inscribed their names on the ruins of Baalbec. "Peters" was a disguise for Twichell in one of the tales that cluttered the "Idle Excursion." Huck Finn used "George Peters" as an alias in one of his many adventures. Emily Kirkham was twenty-five in the spring of 1877, not eighteen. (Her mother died in January 1894. She bequeathed to her youngest daughter the house and lot "situate [*sic*] in Cedar avenue" so long as she remained unmarried.)[12]

Clemens stayed on the Islands only three days: a visit, said the *Royal Gazette*, that was all too brief. But the few days at least revived his affection for Bermuda, and gave him another opportunity to display his white suits. "White clothes—most conspicuous person on the planet—the only grown-up male, savage or civ., who wears clean clothes in cold weather," he once wrote in his notebook. The *Gazette* said he explained his costume to a group of friends gathered at the hotel:

> "I wear these white clothes," he declared, "because they stand as the emblem of the Society of Spotless Purity and Perfection, of which I am President, Vice President, Secretary and General Manager, and, incidentally, the only man in the world fit to be a member."
>
> "But who elected you?" asked his old friend. . . .
>
> "I made my election sure," replied Twain, "by restricting the suffrage to one voter: the result was unanimous."
>
> Consul Greene, who sat near, betrayed a certain incredulity at the moment, but later atoned for his skepticism by gracefully dipping the Stars and Stripes as the famous old humorist with his bright little feminine Secretary at his side leaned over the rail of the departing *Bermudian.* Twain watched the flag as it rose and fell in his honour, then bared his white head and waved a parting salute to the sunlit island, whither, it is hoped, he may often return. He came for a rest and his stay, brief though it was, did him much good.
>
> "I have brought my Secretary with me," he said to Maxwell Greene, "because she knows everything; and I find that I don't know anything."
>
> Twain was never for a moment seen in public without the inevitable cigar, of which he said, in defense of his moderation, that he "never smoked more than one at a time."[13]

The paper appended a poem that compared Mark Twain to King Edward VII and President Theodore Roosevelt. He held *his* throne, the verses ended, *By the power alone / Of pleasing the Saxon race.*

As the ship sailed from the pier, the flag was dipped three times, and the King "lifted his head high and saluted with grave beauty," Miss Lyon wrote. She said the little person at his side was Paddy, a pretty girl from the Upper West Side who had been on the same voyage to the Islands. "We spent most of the day [January 7] on deck—even into the night," Miss Lyon continued. "The King and Mr. Twichell walked up and down, but it wasn't comforting companionship for the King as Mr. T. is so deaf and can only hear when he is shouted at." Paddy Madden evidently amused Clemens, and gave him relief from the reverend.

At sea, he also took refuge in continuing to dictate his autobiography. He spoke of the allure of Bermuda, and the pleasures of voyaging there on a great cruise ship:

> That is a pleasant country—Bermuda—and close by and easy to get to. There is a fine modern steamer admirably officered; there is a table which even the hypercritical could hardly find fault with—not even the hypercritical could find fault with the service on board. . . . Many people flit to that garden winter and spring, and heal their worn minds and bodies in its peaceful serenities and its incomparable climate, and it is strange that the people of our northern coasts go there in mere battalions, instead of in armies. The place is beautiful to the eye; it is clothed in flowers; the roads and the boating are all that can be desired; the hotels are good; the waters and the land are brilliant with spirit-reviving sunshine; the people, whether white, black, or brown, are courteous and kindly beyond the utmost stretch of a New York imagination. If poverty and wretchedness exist, there is no visible evidence of it. There is no rush, no hurry, no money-getting frenzy, no fretting, no complaining, no fussing and quarreling; no telegrams, no daily newspapers, no railroads, no tramways, no subways, no trolleys, no Ls, no Tammany, no Republican party, no Democratic party, no graft, no office-seeking, no elections, no legislatures for sale; hardly a dog, seldom a cat, only one steam-whistle; not a saloon, nobody drunk; no W. C. T. U.; and there is a church and a school on every corner. The spirit of the place is serenity, repose, contentment, tranquility—a marked contrast to the spirit of America, which is embodied in the urgent & mannerless phrase "Come step lively," a phrase which ought to be stamped on our coinage in place of "In God we trust." The former expression is full of character, where as the latter has nothing to recommend it but its bland & self-complacent hypocrisy.

Later, he dictated an addendum:

> What Bermuda can do for a person in three short days, in the way of soothing his spirit and setting him up physically, and in giving his life a

new value by temporarily banishing the weariness and the sordidness out of it, is wonderful. . . . Bronchitis disappears there in twenty-four hours; and [it] is the same with sore throats, and kindred ailments, and they do not return until the patient gets back home; yet Bermuda is neglected; not many Americans visit it. I suppose it is too near by. It costs too little trouble and exertion to get to it. It ought to be as far away as Italy; then we would seek it, no doubt, and be properly thankful for its existence. However, there is this much to be said for Americans; that when they go to Bermuda once, they are quite sure to go again. . . . Consider this—if you are tired, and depressed, and half sick: you can reach that refuge inside of two days, and a week or two there will bring back your youth and the lost sunshine of your life, and stop your doctor's bills for a year.

Winter in Bermuda was indeed "well suited to old age, debility, pulmonary affections, and rheumatism," a senior medical officer with the garrison had written in 1896.[14]

Clemens and his party reached New York on Wednesday morning, January 9. "Please don't say I have been away for my health," he told the press, but of course he had. "I have plenty of health. Indeed, I'll give some of it away." The short visit on the Islands, he said, had allowed him to create a sensation by wearing his white suits.[15] Clemens had already thought of spending more time in Bermuda. "We're going to try to find a house down there," Miss Lyon had written the day after Christmas, "for the King thinks he'd like to spend the summer there. They tell him that the atmosphere is so damp his boots will mildew overnight—but he calmly says—'& suppose they do?'" His doctor advised against the plan, but Clemens later considered two places to stay on the Islands. One house he could have rented for only $125 a month. Eventually, for the summer of 1907, he leased a house in Tuxedo Park, New York, at a cost of $1,500 a month.

Whatever displeasure Clemens felt with Twichell, he concealed it very well except from Miss Lyon. Twichell, in his benign and gentle way, wrote that he had been surprised by the invitation Miss Lyon conveyed:

I was very glad to accept the treat so kindly offered. . . . It was a week of rare enjoyment. The weather was perfect every day: the company altogether delightful, M. T. being in excellent spirits all the while. Together we called on Miss Kirkham in Hamilton, with whose mother we had

lodged on our trip there in 1877. . . . We took several long drives, and a
lovely sail in the water about Hamilton, delighting ourselves in the soft
balmy air, and in viewing again the scenes that had enchanted us thirty
years before.[16]

Clemens returned to his home on Fifth Avenue, resumed idle hours at the billiard table, and, as Miss Lyon put it, smoked "every minute." When his book
Christian Science was published in February, he asked Harper & Brothers to
send a presentation copy to Paddy Madden, at 3 West 104th street. He also took
trouble to send her his portrait. "Tell Paddy we've got some photos," he jotted in
a notebook, "but they're too handsome. So a man is coming in a day or so to
make some natural ones." Clemens had already begun making friends at sea
with little girls.

Soon he felt impelled to make another "flying trip" to Bermuda. As if to imitate Huck Finn—"All I wanted was to go somewheres; all I wanted was a
change"—he planned four days at sea for a stay of only twenty-four hours.[17]
"We should have but one night there, for the *Bermudian* sails every Saturday
from here," Miss Lyon noted on March 11, "but the King won't care. He will
have 5 days away from home." Clemens was suffering from gout, and could not
continue with his autobiographical dictations. Miss Lyon telephoned William
Dean Howells, who politely said he was not planning a trip to the Islands. She
then called Paddy Madden. The invitation "delighted her soul," Miss Lyon wrote.
Clemens mentioned the trip when he wrote his daughter Clara on March 12. "I
have lost interest in everything, & am in deadly need of a change," he said, "&
so Miss Lyon & I decided last night to sail for Bermuda next Saturday & be
gone five days. We invited Paddy, by telephone, to go along with us, & her father has given his consent."

The party of three sailed from New York on March 16. Charles W. Eliot, the
president of Harvard University, was on the same ship, and at sea the next day
Miss Lyon wrote that Paddy "proves a delightful bait for the very nicest men on
board. She sat beside President Eliot and seemed to delight him with her empty
little remarks. She loves ice cream, but not candy, and she never drinks coffee, all
of which she says with a conviction that makes you interested in what she is saying. . . . She says a 5-page prayer to the Virgin 5 times a day when she isn't too
sleepy, and so on and so on, and she is so pretty." Also aboard the *Bermudian*
was Thomas D. Peck, a wealthy industrialist from Pittsfield, Massachusetts, who
joined Mark Twain in conducting a shipboard lottery to benefit the Cottage

Hospital. The only civilian hospital on the Islands, it had opened in March 1894 on Happy Valley Road, not far east of Hamilton, with only eight beds, six for male patients and two for females (FIGS. 36 AND 37). The tiny hospital perpetually needed funds, and routinely drew support from church collections on designated "Hospital Sundays."[18]

Peck was uneasily married to Mary Allen Hulbert Peck, a socialite who usually wintered in Bermuda. This season, she was staying at Inwood, an old house in Paget. In the absence of her husband, she met and enchanted Woodrow Wilson, then the president of Princeton University. Wilson was traveling alone, in search of respite. In precarious health (and, like Clemens, long burdened by a trained Presbyterian conscience), he arrived on January 14, only a week after Clemens left with Twichell, Miss Lyon, and Paddy Madden. Wilson wrote his wife the next day. He said the stone houses were "immaculate with whitewash." Later, he wrote of "the perpetual glare of the sun here upon the shining white streets and houses."[19] Wilson was introduced to Mrs. Peck on February 5, only two days before he left the Islands.

FIGURE 36. Cottage Hospital, Pembroke Parish.

FIGURE 37. Hamilton, 1899, looking west (Coit album, courtesy the Bermuda Archives).

The *Bermudian* docked at Hamilton Harbor on Monday morning, March 18. With so little time to spend on land, Clemens and Miss Lyon had no need to unpack; they would spend the night on board. They rode at once to the Princess Hotel, where Mildred Howells, the daughter of Clemens's old friend, had been staying since the previous Monday. After a sail about the Islands, they took a carriage to Paget and called on Mrs. Peck. She had been at Inwood "all winter through," Miss Lyon noted. Clemens got tired, and retreated to the ship for a nap. That night when they dined at the Princess he grew tired again, Miss Lyon wrote, and "swore at his salad, because he couldn't cut it with a dull-sided fork." Their few hours on the Islands resulted in another absurdity. The same Tuesday edition of the *Royal Gazette* reported Mark Twain's arrival and Mark Twain's departure.

With a new Panama hat purchased at the Trimingham Brothers store, Clemens sailed from Bermuda on Tuesday morning. The trip had been too rushed, and on his arrival in New York the first news he heard was that his old friend Thomas Bailey Aldrich, a poet and author, had died. Aldrich once served as an editor of the *Atlantic Monthly*, and in October 1901 had joined Clemens and Howells in receiving an honorary doctor of letters from Yale University. Clemens appreciated Aldrich as good company, and said he had written "half a dozen small poems which are not surpassed in our language for exquisite grace and beauty and finish." He wrote Mrs. Aldrich on March 29 that it grieved him to have missed the funeral, in Boston. "I was not well," he said, "& was exhausted by the sea-passage, & should have been obliged to take a midnight train." In truth, he detested her. The next year, in an autobiographical segment dated July 3, he called her a self-centered, self-seeking, self-satisfied, honey-worded sham. "I do not believe I could ever learn to like her," he said, "except on a raft at sea with no other provisions in sight."

In continuing his autobiography on March 26, 1907, soon after he returned, Clemens struggled to explain his one-day stay in Bermuda. "I have been taking another vacation—a vacation for which there was no excuse that I can think of," he said, "except that I wanted to get away from work for a while to appease a restlessness which invades my system, now and then, and is perhaps induced by the fact that for thirty-five years I have spent all my winters in idleness, and have not learned to feel natural and at home in winter work." He pondered the death of Aldrich, as well as his own survival at seventy-one. Clemens was pleased when he considered how much of the autobiography he had already dictated. His plan was to distribute parts of the autobiography through his existing books, and thereby protect them with a renewed copyright life of twenty-eight years. Because such a strategy could provide for his daughters, Clemens said, "I do not need to stay here any longer."

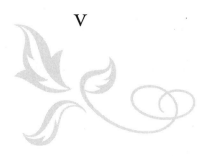

V

RIDING IN A DONKEY CART, 1908

Clemens meant to avoid crossing the Atlantic, but in May 1907 a cablegram from Whitelaw Reid, the publisher of the *Tribune* and now the ambassador to the Court of St. James, revived his spirits and instantly changed his mind. He was to be awarded an honorary degree from Oxford University on June 26. "I take the same childlike delight in a new degree that an Indian takes in a fresh scalp," he said, in expanding his autobiography on May 23, "and I take no more pains to conceal my joy than the Indian does." For a generation he had been as widely celebrated as any literary figure the United States ever produced, he said, and thus had good reason to resent the honors bestowed on "persons of small and temporary consequence." No man surpassed Mark Twain in acknowledging his own vanity:

In these past thirty-five or forty years I have seen our universities distribute nine or ten thousand honorary degrees and overlook me every time. Of all those thousands, not fifty were known outside of America, and not a hundred are still famous in it. This neglect would have killed a less robust person than I am, but it has not killed me; it has only shortened my life and weakened my constitution; but I shall get my strength back now. Out of those decorated and forgotten thousands not more than ten have been decorated by Oxford, and I am quite well aware—and so is America, and so is the rest of Christendom—that an Oxford decoration is a

loftier distinction than is conferrable by any other university on either
side of the ocean.

In fact, he had already received two honorary degrees from Yale and one from
the University of Missouri.

After failing to enlist George Harvey for the voyage, Clemens hired Ralph
Ashcroft as his special traveling secretary. Ashcroft, an Englishman, had served
as the New York agent for Plasmon, one of Clemens's many ill-advised investments. Plasmon, advertised as a fat-free, sugar-free concentrate in milk, claimed
to be twenty times more nutritious than the milk itself, and thus eminently
suited to invigorate both the body and the nerves. Later, after Ashcroft began to
manage the King's business affairs, he was obliged to play cards and to operate
the Aeolian orchestrelle, a contraption for providing the household with musical
entertainment. In return, Clemens called him by various pet names: Ashcot,
Ashpan, Ashhopper, the Lord Bishop of Benares, or simply Benares, after the
holy city in India he had described in *Following the Equator* as "a strange and
fascinating piety-hive" reputedly peopled with more stone lingams than inhabitants.[1] Ashcroft was a slight, bearded, ascetic-looking man; he had "a good theo-
logical head," Clemens said.

On June 8 they sailed for England on the *Minneapolis,* and Clemens began to
pursue young shipmates. Two months earlier he had invited Paddy Madden to a
dinner party at 21 Fifth Avenue, where Miss Lyon again found her "pretty and
absolutely empty-headed." His great catch for companionship in England was
Frances Nunnally, a handsome girl from Atlanta. She attended a finishing school
in Catonsville, Maryland. Miss Lyon wrote that she was "a dear grave girl of 16,
with the most wonderful little slender hands." Clemens soon romanticized her
name into "Francesca." They enjoyed a whirl of social calls and events in London, and in her old age Francesca treasured the double portrait they posed for in
Knightsbridge, Hyde Park Corner (FIG. 38).[2]

Clemens was still the man his wife had called "Youth." But besides illness, he
experienced another penalty of prolonged age. Old friends died, and younger
ones were too busy to take time for spontaneous travels or heroically long hours
at billiards. Orion, his brother, had observed many years earlier that Sam was
given to extremes of feeling, and now the feeling was loneliness. His surviving
daughters were grown and often gone. The little adventures with schoolgirls, somewhat poignant and evidently harmless, attested to his renown, good manners,
charm, and—not the least—his abiding admiration for childhood. His young

FIGURE 38. "Francesca" (Frances Nunnally) and Clemens, London, July 9, 1907 (courtesy the Huntington Library).

companions relieved boredom and his longstanding rage at what he called the insects and reptiles of "the damned human race"—not in an expression of piety, Howells hastened to point out. (Mark Twain's protagonist in *A Connecticut Yankee in King Arthur's Court* speaks of times "when one would like to hang the whole human race and finish the farce.") Clemens also liked how girls looked. When he peered down from the speakers' platform at Vassar College he saw a "great garden of young and lovely blossoms," and to a correspondent in France who sent him a picture of Joan of Arc he wrote that nothing else in the world "is ever so beautiful as a beautiful schoolgirl."[3]

Clemens's lighthearted pursuit of schoolgirls grew more consuming in his last few trips to Bermuda. Typically, the girls came from well-to-do families, went to private schools, and traveled almost always with their mothers. In an autobiographical segment dictated on April 17, 1908, Clemens spoke of the "little people whom I worship":

> After my wife's death, June 5, 1904, I experienced a long period of unrest & loneliness. Clara & Jean were busy with their studies & their labors, & I was washing about on a forlorn sea of banquets & speechmaking in high & holy causes—industries which furnished me intellectual cheer & entertainment, but got at my heart for an evening only, then left it dry and dusty. I had reached the grandpapa stage of life; & what I lacked & what I needed, was grandchildren, but I didn't know it. By & by this knowledge came. . . . In grandchildren I am the richest man that lives to-day; for I *select* my grandchildren, whereas all other grandfathers have to take them as they come, good, bad, & indifferent.

Clemens also sought companions among adults. On the way to England, he met the young polymath Archibald Henderson, a professor of mathematics who planned to write a biography of George Bernard Shaw. They arrived on June 18 and took the boat train from the Tilbury docks to St. Pancras Station in London, where Shaw stood waiting. Henderson introduced Mark Twain to Shaw, who already ranked him as one of the two greatest American writers, the other being Edgar Allan Poe. (In a famous letter to Howells, early in 1909, Clemens wrote that Poe's prose, like Jane Austen's, was unreadable. "No, there is a difference," he added. "I could read his prose on salary, but not Jane's. Jane is entirely impossible. It seems a great pity that they allowed her to die a natural death.") Clemens already knew his reputation in England. A cablegram to celebrate his seventieth birthday bore the names of Thomas Hardy, George Meredith, G. K. Chesterton, Edmund Gosse, Arthur Conan Doyle, J. M. Barrie, Rudyard Kipling, and George Trevelyan. A few years later, Henderson published a biography in which he wrote that Mark Twain "comprehensively incorporated and realized his own country and his own age as no American has so completely done before him."[4]

Busy days of meetings and speeches and parties occupied Clemens in England for nearly a month. He was in his element. The pageantry at Oxford, he said, could provide hints for his own funeral. "I think this funeral is going to be a great thing," Clemens remarked. "I shall be there." On June 22 he appeared at a garden party at Windsor Castle, a special guest of King Edward VII. By the time of the ceremonies at Oxford he had attracted more attention than Kipling, Auguste Rodin, Camille Saint-Saens, or Gen. William Booth of the Salvation Army, all fellow honorees. Before he left on the *Minnetonka,* on July 13, he prepared a message to the press. "I have led a violently gay and energetic life for four weeks," Clemens said. "I am younger now by seven years than I was, and if I could stay another month I could make it fourteen."[5]

Miss Lyon was waiting on the pier when the ship reached New York on July 22. Clemens was standing on the lower deck, she wrote later, "with a little girl snuggling up against him." He had met Dorothy Quick, not yet eleven, soon after the steamship sailed from England. She, too, suffered from bronchitis, but what particularly endeared her to Clemens was her desire to become a writer. In continuing his autobiography on October 5, he said it was a privilege "to egg her on, and beguile her into working her imagination." Clemens marveled at her untutored way of writing, rushed and vigorous and wholly lacking in punctuation. Dorothy had a governess, and that fall would enter school for the first time. Grammar came eventually. In later years, she wrote numerous books. One was titled *Enchantment: A Little Girl's Friendship with Mark Twain.*

Soon after his return, Clemens took ill. He importuned George Harvey. "I am in bed again & out of temper," he wrote another friend on July 29. "Harvey is coming this evening. He & I were going to Bermuda to-morrow for a couple of weeks, but it turns out that he can't. He thinks Deal Beach [in New Jersey, where Harvey had a summer place] will set me up, & so I am to go there." He also asked Robert J. Collier, the editor and publisher of *Collier's Weekly,* to join him for a voyage to Bermuda. That, too, fell through. Having declared himself "an innocent old dilapidation," he invited Francesca and little Dorothy Quick, who lived in Plainfield, New Jersey, to be house guests at Tuxedo Park, where they could play games, read aloud, and such.[6] They would be attended by Miss Lyon, whom he described as a woman in her forties with experience as a governess. Dorothy arrived early in August for a visit of four days. "What is a home without a child?" Clemens wrote after she left on August 9. "It isn't a home at all, it's merely a wreck." When she visited him again in September they formed an "Authors' League" of only two members. Clemens told her she faced a "long & diligent apprenticeship—not anything short of 10 years." Later in the month, Francesca and her mother paid him a weekend visit.

That fall, Clemens commented that religion was of no use to him. He told a Christian Scientist that no religion or god ever invented by man could lay claim to the respect of thinking people. "But people don't think, anyway," he said. "They only feel." At the same time, he was perfecting a new tale for his platform repertoire. He had encountered Gen. Nelson Appleton Miles on March 12 at a luncheon in New York, and on October 3 he dictated his great story of General Miles and the three-dollar dog. He told it first in a performance at Tuxedo Park on October 22, a few days before he moved the household back to 21 Fifth Avenue. Mark Twain repeated the story for a private dinner party at the Players Club, and for a banquet audience at the Pleiades Club on December 22, when Dorothy Quick sat with him at the head table. He had proved that he could bring fresh life into the forlorn sea of banquets and speech making, and he would again relate the saga of the three-dollar dog the next spring, in Bermuda.[7] At the end of the year, other banquets feted his friend Howells, who was about to leave for Italy. When a young man, Howells served as the U.S. consul in Venice during the Civil War years.

"I wish you were here," Clemens wrote Francesca on December 29, "so that I could have you at dinner this evening & show you off, as I did to those admiring families in London." He was struggling to keep amused, because winters in New York often threatened his spirits as much as his health. Clemens tried to launch a "Human Race Luncheon Club" for stag gatherings at his home, and early in January 1908 he complained to Miss Lyon that life was so empty he couldn't even stage a game of billiards when he felt like it. Tired of banquets, he had taken to arriving late and leaving early. "A banquet is probably the most fatiguing thing in the world except ditchdigging," he said. When honored at a Lotos Club affair on January 11, he stayed long enough to talk about a time forty-two years earlier. He was engaged to lecture in a log schoolhouse, Mark Twain said, to an audience of gold miners. Someone had to introduce him, and they chose a miner, who objected and said, "I don't know anything about this man, anyway. I only know two things about him. One is, he has never been in jail; and the other is, I don't know why."[8]

In response to a mildly feminist scolding about his "buck" luncheons, Clemens arranged a "doe" event on January 14 for nine of his married women friends. His daughter Clara and Miss Lyon also attended, if only to lend an air of propriety. On each place card, Clemens drew a small deer. A few days later, he drank a great deal of whisky to cure a cold. That night he played his favorite card game, Hearts, until after three o'clock in the morning. The next night he was still playing billiards with Albert Bigelow Paine, his official biographer, at two thirty in the morning. "That whisky came very handy," Clemens wrote to his friend Andrew Carnegie, who was supplying him with a private label of Scotch. "I had a very wild and exasperating cold, but a pint of the whisky tamed it in 3 minutes by the watch—I did not wake up again for ten hours." He told Julia O. Langdon, the daughter of Charlie Langdon, that he was using whisky to avert bronchitis. "I dread a cold as the Presbyterian burnt child dreads perdition," he wrote her on January 16.

Two days later, his old friend Edmund Clarence Stedman, the poet and critic, died unexpectedly. "Lord grant me his good fortune to slip suddenly out of the tragedy of life unwarned," Clemens wrote. In dictating more of his autobiography on the following July 3, he said Stedman was a good fellow but "believed that the sun merely rose to admire his poetry & was so reluctant to set at the end of the day & lose sight of it, that it lingered & lingered & lost many minutes diurnally & was never able to keep correct time during his stay in the earth." Stedman, in turn, had complained twenty years earlier that so far as an author making a decent income, "not every one can be, like Mr. Clemens, his own Harper & Brothers, and his own Edwin Booth."[9]

Clemens tried again without success to get Robert Collier and his wife to join him for a trip to Bermuda. He reverted to Ralph Ashcroft, but would have preferred a schoolgirl. "I wish you were here & had 2 weeks to spare," he wrote Francesca on January 21. "Then I would pack you & Miss Lyon aboard ship & sail for Bermuda. . . . I shall take nobody but Ashcroft—yet he hasn't any use for a voyage." He wrote Dorothy Quick the same day:

Dorothy dear, tell your mother that the wisest way for her to spend money on your health will be to take you to Bermuda for a week or a fortnight; & you must tell her that the best *time* is next Saturday. (That is because I am going there, then, & so is Ashcroft.) It's the big ship (the "Bermudian"). She makes the passage across in 45 hours.

> In Bermuda a sick person gets well in 3 days & strong in a week. . . . I tried the trip twice last year, & I know—the change made me well in 3 days.
>
> The doctors say I shall be well enough by Saturday [January 25] to sail— so Mr. Ashcroft has secured the staterooms.
>
> I hope you are well by this time, dear. You only need the Bermuda air to make you weller than ever you were in your life before.

As planned, Clemens sailed with Ashcroft on Saturday, and in spite of stormy seas the *Bermudian* docked in Hamilton Harbor on Monday morning. Just as he had predicted, his vigor quickly returned (FIG. 39). In only a week on the Islands, he made new friends (some were schoolgirls), conversed in Somerset with the writer Upton Sinclair, and dined in Paget with Mrs. Peck and Woodrow Wilson. Although given to grumbling about "the damned human race," Clemens treated individuals with grace and respect. In that way, as in so many others, he was like Jonathan Swift; despite detesting "that animal called man," Swift wrote Alexander Pope, "I heartily love John, Peter, Thomas, and so forth."[10] Clemens already knew some of the other tourists. "We are very comfortably located," he wrote Clara, "in the new addition to the Princess, with private bathroom, etc. The weather is balmy & sunny & altogether satisfactory. The hotels are full of people, & a shark has been seen in the Bay. There is no other society-news."

Elizabeth Wallace, a woman of formidable accomplishments, had arrived at the hotel on December 30 for a long winter holiday. She was a professor of French literature and dean at the University of Chicago. On January 3 she began a journal. "Here there is quiet and peace, cleanliness and repose," she wrote. "The atmosphere is so pure, the water is so transparent, the sky so clear that surely it will be easier to understand truth here. There can be little place for sham or pose or insincerity." Miss Wallace, who was traveling with her invalid mother, Martha T. Wallace of Minneapolis, was playing a game called Diablo one day on the veranda of the hotel when she met Margaret Blackmer, a school-girl from New York. Margaret had been in Bermuda since December 9. She was traveling with *her* invalid mother and was "a lovely looking child of twelve," Miss Wallace wrote, "tall and slim and dark with a very straight nose and very straight hair." She wore short dresses, Miss Wallace noted, that "exposed a pair of very long slender legs." The two became companions in playing Diablo and taking long walks.[11]

Younger guests left the hotel for the harbor whenever a cruise ship was docking,

FIGURE 39. Clemens with "Benares" (Ralph Ashcroft) in Bermuda, 1908 (courtesy the Mark Twain Project, the Bancroft Library).

Miss Wallace said, then returned to the veranda to scrutinize every carriage of arriving tourists. A few years later, she began her memoir *Mark Twain and the Happy Island* by telling of her first sight of Clemens:

The road to the hotel wound upward, and on either side of it palmettos rustled noisily beside still and somber cedars.

Out from under their shadows stepped a gray figure with a crown of glistening white hair. He walked lightly and looked about him with an air of interested and unconscious expectancy. As he came nearer the hotel veranda we recognized the shaggy eyebrows, the delicately arched nose, the drooping mustache. . . .

As a usual thing, Margaret and I felt but a languid interest in the passengers who came, for they did not invade our world. But on the morning that Mark Twain arrived, we felt an unusual thrill. . . .

Margaret's table was not far from ours, and that day she was sitting alone. Presently Mark Twain came in, and as he reached her table he stopped and spoke to her. He not only spoke to her, but had a conversation with her. I knew, then, that he had recognized her as one of the choice souls of the earth.[12]

Clemens had asked Margaret to ride with him that afternoon in a donkey cart. He knew she was only twelve, and told her that by the almanac he was seventy-two; otherwise, he said, he was still fourteen. In an autobiographical passage dictated on February 13, he said his first day in Bermuda paid a double dividend, for "it broke the back of my cold and it added a jewel to my collection." He continued:

We were close comrades—inseparables in fact—for eight days. Every day we made pedestrian excursions—called them that any way, and honestly they were intended for that, and that is what they would have been but for the persistent intrusion of a gray and grave and rough-coated little donkey by the name of Maude. Maude was four feet long; she was mounted on four slender little stilts, and had ears that doubled her altitude when she stood them up straight. Which she seldom did. Her ears were a most interesting study. She was always expressing her private thoughts and opinions with them, and doing it with such nice shadings, and so intelligibly, that she had no need of speech whereby to reveal her mind. This was all new to me. The donkey had always been a sealed book to me before, but now I saw that I could read this one as easily as I could read coarse print. Sometimes she would throw those ears straight forward, like the prongs of a fork; under the impulse of a fresh emotion she would lower the starboard one to a level; next she would stretch it backward till it pointed nor'-nor'east; next she would retire it to due east, and presently clear down to southeast-by-south—all these changes revealing her thoughts to me without her suspecting it. She always worked the port ear for a quite different set of emotions, and sometimes she would fetch both ears rearward till they were level and became a fork, the one prong pointing southeast, the other southwest. She was a most interesting little creature, and always self-possessed, always dignified, always resisting authority; never in agreement with anybody, and if she ever smiled once during the eight days I did not catch her at it. Her tender was a little bit of a cart with seat room for two in it, and you could fall out of it without knowing it, it was so close to the ground. This battery was in command of a nice grave, dignified, gentle-faced little black boy whose age was about twelve, and whose name, for some reason or other, was Reginald. Reginald and Maude—I shall not easily forget those gorgeous names, nor the combination they stood for.

On earlier excursions with Twichell he had favored the North Shore and its unimpeded vistas toward the ocean. A deep Mediterranean blue, Mark Twain had written, was "about the divinest color known to nature," and its beauty could break the heart. The sparkle of the sea was like that of diamonds. "Nothing is so beautiful," he wrote in *Following the Equator,* "as a rose diamond with the light playing through it, except that uncostly thing which is just like it—wavy seawater with the sunlight playing through it and striking a white-sand bottom."[13] Riding in the donkey cart, Clemens usually meandered northwest to Spanish Point, so known since the settlers early in the seventeenth century discovered evidence of Spanish castaways. Topographically considered, Spanish Point gave shape to the Great Sound and protected Hamilton Harbor. It also offered broad views that encompassed Ireland Island and the Dockyard (FIG. 40). The same tranquil scene that Clemens enjoyed was captured a few years earlier by Winslow Homer, in a watercolor.[14] From the autobiography, again:

The excursioning party always consisted of the same persons: Miss W[allace], Margaret, Reginald, Maude and me. The trip out & return was five or six miles, and it generally took us three hours to make it. This was because Maude set the pace. She had the finest eye in the company for an ascending grade; she could detect an ascending grade where neither water nor a spirit-level could do it, and whenever she detected an ascending grade she respected it; she stopped and said with her ears,

FIGURE 40. Vista from Spanish Point, Pembroke Parish.

"This is getting unsatisfactory. We will camp here."

Then all the vassals would get behind the cart and shove it up the ascending grade, and shove Maude along with it. The whole idea of these excursions was that Margaret and I should employ them for the gathering of strength, by walking—yet we were oftener in the cart than out of it. She drove and I superintended. In the course of the first excursion I found a beautiful little shell on the beach at Spanish Point; its hinge was old and dry, and the two halves came apart in my hand. I gave one of them to Margaret and said,

"Now dear, sometime or other in the future I shall run across you somewhere, and it may turn out that it is not you at all, but some girl that only resembles you. I shall be saying to myself, 'I know that this is a Margaret, by the look of her, but I don't know for sure whether this is my Margaret or somebody else's'; but no matter, I can soon find out, for I shall take my half-shell out of my pocket and say, 'I think you are my Margaret, but I am not certain; if you are my Margaret you will be able to produce the other half of this shell.'"

Next morning when I entered the breakfast-room and saw the child sitting solitary at her two-seated breakfast-table I approached and scanned her searchingly all over, then said sadly,

"No, I am mistaken; she looks like my Margaret, but she isn't, and I am sorry. I will go away and cry, now."

Her eyes danced triumphantly, and she cried out,

"No, you don't have to. There!" and she fetched out the identifying shell.

I was beside myself with gratitude and joyful surprise, and revealed it from every pore. The child could not have enjoyed this thrilling little drama more if we had been playing it on the stage. Many times afterward she played the chief part herself, pretending to be in doubt as to my identity and challenging me to produce my half of the shell. She was always hoping to catch me without it, but I always defeated that game—wherefore she came at last to recognize that I was not only old, but very smart.

Miss Wallace also recounted the seashell episode, but in an unimaginative and probably more factual way. "It was Mr. Clemens's greatest joy to start off for a tramp with Margaret and his faithful Mr. Ashcroft and sometimes one or two others," she wrote in her journal. She thought Ashcroft looked like her youngest brother, and said he usually walked in front of the donkey; hence Clemens called him the "Pilot Fish." Miss Wallace discerned that Clemens was trying to recover an earlier time of his life. "He had a yearning fondness for children and especially for young girls between ten and sixteen," she wrote, "for it was during those years that he had as his constant companion his little daughter Susy—whose loss still seems an open wound after all these years."[15]

Woodrow Wilson had been on the Islands since January 20. The day before he arrived, he twisted his left knee in a fall on shipboard. Wilson was staying at the Hamilton Hotel, on the hill. He found it "plain but very comfortable." Wilson wrote his wife that the Hamilton competed with the Princess even in baseball games, the teams indiscriminately formed of guests and employees. "There is no one in the hotel who is very remarkable," he wrote, "but a sufficient number of pleasant people to form an enjoyable circle. Young and gay people for the most part go to the other hotel: this one is the favourite resort of sedate middle-aged persons like myself. I feel *very* sedate and middle-aged at this remove from my field of battle, and look upon myself with a sort of half sad amusement." Naively, he told of how excited he was to find his new friend on the Islands. "I have seen Mrs. Peck twice," he said, "and really she is very fine. You must know her." Wilson wrote that Mrs. Peck had an interesting mind and a frank and open disposition. Then he complained:

> Now I am cut out by Mark Twain! He arrived on the boat this morning, and Mrs. Peck at once took possession of him [FIG. 41]. They are old friends. Indeed, she seems to know everybody that is worth knowing. She has been coming down here a great many winters, and everybody turns up here sooner or later, it would seem. I have not yet found out where Mr. Clemons [*sic*] is staying. I hoped he was coming to the Hamilton, but he went off in another direction. I did not get a chance to speak to him, and do not know whether he would remember me or not.[16]

FIGURE 41. Mrs. Peck with Clemens at Shoreby, 1908 (courtesy the Mark Twain Project, the Bancroft Library).

Wilson had hosted a luncheon for his inauguration as president of Princeton on October 25, 1902, that was attended by Clemens, Howells, and J. P. Morgan, among others. The year before, when Yale University celebrated its bicentennial, he and Clemens and Howells were among those awarded honorary degrees, on October 23.

Wilson saw the vivacious Mrs. Peck as often as he could. She was staying again in Paget Parish, but this season at a house named Shoreby, directly across the harbor from Hamilton. Mrs. Peck had named her dog Paget Montmorenci Vere de Vere. Needless to say, Paget was the center of social status and snobbery. Mrs. Peck believed herself to be an entirely different woman when she wintered on the Islands. "Joyous, with an almost pagan delight in basking in its beauty, its sunshine and freshness," she wrote later, "I felt at home in Bermuda."[17] Wilson repaired to Shoreby almost every day, to take tea and rest his knee. Mrs. Peck felt honored by his continuing adoration, but said his manner was somewhat stilted and puritanical, and he reminded her of the Reverend Phillips Brooks, the famous Episcopal clergyman in Boston. Wilson liked to label people either good or bad, she wrote, and did not smoke or swim or dance. ("I haven't a particle of confidence in a man who has no redeeming petty vices," Mark Twain wrote many years earlier.)[18] One day, Wilson toured the new Bermuda aquarium as a guest of Louis L. Mowbray, the founding curator. Mrs. Peck said he mistook a stone to be a naked mollusk.

Clemens and Wilson shared a spicy meal at Shoreby, but at coffee Wilson's high-minded talk about government left Clemens bored. They remained on friendly terms, and Clemens readily signed a petition Wilson drafted in opposition to any proliferation of motorcars on the Islands:

> We, the undersigned, visitors to Bermuda, venture respectfully to express the opinion that the admission of automobiles to the island would alter the whole character of the place. . . .
>
> The island now attracts visitors in considerable numbers because of the quiet and dignified simplicity of its life. It derives its principal charm from its utter detachment from the world of strenuous business and feverish pleasure in which most of us are obliged to spend the greater part of our time. . . . [W]e are confident that the free introduction of such vehicles, especially by visitors, would in the mind of everyone capable of appreciating the natural and wholesome pleasures of the place make it a place to shun rather than to resort to. . . .

The danger to be apprehended is chiefly from reckless tourists who would care nothing for local opinion or for the convenience and safety of others. This is one of the last refuges now left in the world to which one can come to escape such persons. It would, in our opinion, be a fatal error to attract to Bermuda the extravagant and sporting set who have made so many other places of pleasure entirely intolerable to persons of taste and cultivation.[19]

Well trained in controversy, Wilson correctly gauged how heated the issue had become. His arguments were sound and appealing. A rabid letter signed "Americus" appeared in the *Royal Gazette* a few days later:

There is little doubt that the automobile is the worst affliction that has cursed the world since the beginning of civilization.

The cruelties of the Spanish Inquisition had some justification because they were supposed to be necessary for the salvation of souls, but there is no possible excuse for the use of the mercilessly murderous automobiles because they are employed solely for the personal gratification of individuals whose frenzied desire for pleasure cannot be satisfied without the excitement of some pursuit which will bring them continuously face to face with danger to life and limb.

They are so frightfully dangerous that their use ought to be considered an attack upon the welfare of society, and every operator should be instantly apprehended under the common law on a charge of criminal recklessness. . . .

It is a curious obsession. In many instances homes and farms are mortgaged to obtain the means for the gratification of the monstrous passion.[20]

Wilson's petition and the polemic from Americus helped curb the monstrous passion, and private automobiles were banned by a law not repealed until 1946. (The Bermuda Railway, which began service in 1931, expired in 1948. Cars today are limited to four cylinders, with only one car to a household. Although the speed limit is thirty-five kilometers, or less than twenty-two miles, an hour, cars remain ill-suited to the curved and narrow roads, which are crowded by stone walls and plant life, threatened by concealed entrances, and rarely graced by shoulders or sidewalks. Motor scooters flourish. At most places on the Islands, the peace and quiet that Clemens so appreciated is attained only on weekend mornings.)

Other aspects of modern life had come under attack from Upton Sinclair, the firebrand socialist writer. He arrived in Bermuda on December 20, 1907, for a stay of six months. Only twenty-nine, Sinclair had already published his best-known book, *The Jungle,* an outcry against working conditions at the Chicago stockyards. He sent a copy to Clemens, who responded that he realized the magnitude and effectiveness of the earthquake it caused under the "Polecat Trust of Chicago." Clemens raged in his autobiography about Sinclair's exposure of "the most titanic & death-dealing swindle of them all, the Beef Trust." He added, "I believe the entire population of the United States—exclusive of the women—to be rotten, as far as the dollar is concerned." Having spurred the passage of the Pure Food and Drug Act, which President Roosevelt signed in June 1906, Sinclair temporarily became a vegetarian. In Bermuda he collaborated with Michael Williams, a fellow socialist, in writing a book about good health. Together with family members and servants, their entourage numbered twelve persons. Sinclair wrote about his domestic scene in Somerset, at the West End:

> The house is white limestone, set upon a rocky shore overlooking a little bay, behind which the sun sets every evening. Out on a point in front of us there stands an old ruin of a mansion, deserted, but having a marvelous mahogany staircase inside, so that we can assure the children it was once the home of a pirate chief. The water is brilliant azure, shading to emerald in the shallows; over it flies the man-o'-war's bird, snow-white, with a long white feather trailing like a pennant. The sun shines nearly always. There is a tennis-court, surrounded by a towering hedge of oleanders in perpetual blossom. There are roses, and a garden in which a colored boy raises our vegetarian vegetables. The house is wide and rambling, with enough verandas so that both halves of this two-family Utopia can sleep outdoors.[21]

Clemens went to see Sinclair, the *Royal Gazette* reported, but the carriage ride to Somerset took so long they had no time for a vegetarian dinner. Although he did "not go to the length of declaring himself a vegetarian," the paper said, Clemens was "in the habit of curing occasional ailments by total abstinence from meat during periods of a week or more at a time." Much later, in *Mammonart,* a self-published study of the arts in relation to the class struggle, Sinclair said Clemens had been America's uncrowned king. He recalled their brief meeting in Bermuda. "He had taken to wearing a conspicuous white costume," Sinclair wrote, "and with his snow-white hair and mustache he was a picturesque figure. He chatted about past times, as old men like to do. I saw that he was kind, warm-hearted, and also full of rebellion against capitalist greed and knavery; but he was an old man, and a sick man, and I did not try to probe the mystery of his life."[22]

Keeping company with a schoolgirl always brightened Clemens's day. In his hours with Margaret Blackmer he cheerfully devised games based on historical facts about royalty. By drawing odd or grotesque images with extra arms and legs, ears, or toes, he contrived to signify how many years a monarch reigned. The games, meant to be educational, were much like those he played in the summer of 1883 with his own daughters. Clemens once hoped to market them on a vast and lucrative scale, another of his pipe dreams. But he amused Margaret and enthralled Miss Wallace:

> In the delight of knowing Mr. Clemens we almost forgot Mark Twain. This charming, courteous gentleman, with the crown of silver hair, with his immaculate white clothes, his kindly deference of manner, his ready thoughtfulness, and his sweet affection for children, was sufficient in himself to win anyone's heart. . . .

> The dining-room was a large light room overlooking the sea. The meals were leisurely to the last degree, and it was a very nice place in which to make informal calls. Mr. Clemens was rather abstemious, and when he had finished earlier than the rest of us he would often come over to our table and talk. His whimsical way of putting things, his deep knowledge of human nature, his half-pessimistic philosophy, his kindly toleration, in most things, made everything he said so precious that we did not want to lose a word.[23]

Miss Wallace listened as he compared youth to advanced age. Youth held everything precious about this weary life; old age was a wanton insult. Paine, his biographer, wrote that Clemens liked to say:

> If I had been helping the Almighty when He created man, I would have had Him begin at the other end, and start human beings with old age.

How much better it would have been to start old and have all the bitterness and blindness of age in the beginning! One would not mind then if
he were looking forward to a joyful youth. Think of the joyous prospect
of growing young instead of old! Think of looking forward to eighteen
instead of eighty! Yes, the Almighty made a poor job of it. I wish He had
invited my assistance.[24]

Forward to eighteen, perhaps, but memories of his childhood left Clemens in a
conflict he never quite resolved. By his own account, the lives of Tom Sawyer
and Huckleberry Finn in those old and simple times were pervaded by ignorance, superstition, fantasy, and a devotion to sentimental, storybook romance.
They were beset as well by the restraints of school, church, parents, and the
trained Presbyterian conscience. Could childhood years of illusion and distress
surpass a healthy skepticism and its wiser, if sadder, grasp of the world?

By now, the *Royal Gazette* paid better attention to Mark Twain and other lu-
minaries on the Islands. "I wanted to stay in Bermuda another week," he told a
reporter on Monday afternoon, February 3, just before the *Bermudian* set sail,
"but I have an important engagement for next week that must be kept." It was
only another doe luncheon, set for February 11. Clemens promised to return to
Bermuda soon, and to stay longer. He talked about his voyage to accept the
honorary degree from Oxford. In England, he said, he took special pride in the
cheers from stevedores, who recognized him standing on the deck of the steamship.[25]

The ship reached New York on Thursday. Miss Lyon was pleased to see Clemens
looking so healthy and happy, "with pink cheeks and a beautiful 'spring in his
hind-legs.'" Despite the range of his amusements, he remained prey to dark
thoughts. For the doe luncheon on February 11 he sent a special invitation to
Dorothea Gilder, the daughter of Richard Watson Gilder, editor of *Scribner's
Monthly* and its successor, the *Century*. Clemens drew a small stick-figure scene,
and titled it "Ship sinking—man overboard." But in a letter to Charlie Langdon
he said that doing nothing in Bermuda had been "good & satisfactory medicine
for me—the best I know of." On February 12 he expanded his autobiography:

I have been to Bermuda again; this is the fifth time; it was on account of
bronchitis, my annual visitor for these seventeen or eighteen years. I have
not come out of any previous attack so quickly or so pleasantly. . . . We
made the passage in forty-five hours and landed in lovely summer weather.

The passage itself came near to curing me, for a radical change is a good doctor. A single day of constant and delightful exposure to the Bermudian sun completed the cure; then I stayed seven days longer to enjoy the spiritual serenities and the bodily rejuvenations furnished by that happy little paradise. It grieves me, and I feel reproached, that I allowed the physicians to send Mrs. Clemens on a horrible ten-day sea journey to Italy when Bermuda was right here at hand and worth a hundred Italies, for her needs. . . . [F]or climate Florence was a sarcasm as compared with Bermuda.

I suppose we are all collectors. . . . As for me, I collect pets: young girls— girls from ten to sixteen years old; girls who are pretty and sweet and naive and innocent—dear young creatures to whom life is a perfect joy and to whom it has brought no wounds, no bitterness, and few tears. My collection consists of gems of the first water.

VI

THE GRAND RETURN

In her daybook for February 1908, Miss Lyon wrote of the "Great Lonely Sorrow of the King's life." She saw that as Clemens grew older he became lonelier. "The King's interest in children increases—his interest in little girls," she wrote on February 8, when Dorothy Quick arrived for another weekend visit at 21 Fifth Avenue. "He can spend hours and hours with them and finds them such good company." Before he sailed home, Clemens asked Miss Wallace to find a potential successor to Margaret Blackmer, who left on the same ship. He also carried back presents for Dorothy and Francesca. The gift for Francesca he described as a pin "decorated with an image of Bermuda's pride, the angel-fish." Clemens had associated angelfish with attractive girls perhaps as early as 1877, when he and Twichell visited Devil's Hole. Big eyes, pouty lips, and lovely colors were all points of comparison. He was hardly alone in such perceptions. Julia Dorr saw "something so human in their mild, innocent faces," and William Dean Howells wrote of their "transparent purity of substance" and their "cherubic innocence of expression."[1]

True to his word, Clemens returned to Bermuda later in February and stayed much longer than ever before, forty-seven days. Evidently bored with Ashcroft, he gathered a larger group: his close friend Henry Huttleston Rogers, of the Standard Oil Trust; William E. Benjamin, who was Rogers's son-in-law; the loyal Miss Lyon; and Rogers's valet. He insisted that the trip was not for his own health, but to benefit Rogers. As if he needed to prove so, Clemens expanded his autobiography on February 19 by talking about a party given by Robert Collier. "I was at home by half-past four in the morning, in bed at five, asleep at six, and ready for breakfast at eight—refreshed and ready for more activities," he said. "It is as I said, I am not leaving for Bermuda to build up my health, for there is nothing the matter with it; I am going because a change of scene and climate is absolutely necessary for H. H. Rogers, and he won't go unless I go too." When they sailed on February 22, Miss Lyon wrote that "Mr. Rogers came feebly onto the boat, a sick, sick man."

H. H. ("Hell Hound") Rogers—a hound of hell had been famously portrayed in 1901 by Arthur Conan Doyle in *The Hound of the Baskervilles*—was a multimillionaire commonly considered a ruthless predator. He admired Mark Twain's book *Roughing It,* and once said, "As the man who sold two-cent cigars at sixty cents apiece in his shack in the middle of the alkali desert remarked: 'We are not in business for our health.'"[2] But now his health indeed had failed; he suffered a stroke in July 1907. Rogers had begun to manage Clemens's financial affairs in 1893. Although his time was worth thousands of dollars a day, said the *World's Work,* he served Clemens entirely in friendship, guiding him out of bankruptcy into substantial new wealth. Ambivalent in his attitude toward the very rich, Clemens joked about the "Standard Oiligarchy" and recalled how much cod-liver oil he had been fed as a child, saying, "I was the first Standard Oil Trust."[3]

On board the *Bermudian* and surrounded by newspapermen, the two old-timers made light of the disparity in their reputations. "This is what I get for being in bad company," Clemens said as he pointed toward Rogers. "My methods," Rogers responded, "are no worse than your jokes."[4] They arrived in Hamilton on Monday, February 24, and registered at the Princess Hotel. The most public of all Clemens's visits to the Islands began slowly. He found his room so small he declared it a former cigar box, and because the day was rainy, he and Rogers abandoned their plan of riding to Shoreby to see Mrs. Peck and Woodrow Wilson, who was spending his last day on the Islands. Miss Wallace, still on holiday, found it a mooted question whether Rogers was taking care of Clemens, or Clemens of Rogers (FIG. 42). She also wondered about the relation between Clemens and his secretary. Miss Lyon was "a black eyed black haired Italian looking little woman," she wrote in her Bermuda journal, "who hovers about him with the tender care of a mother and daughter combined." Surprisingly, the two women became friends. Miss Wallace nevertheless made certain that the King found company with Irene Gerken, a pert little twelve year old from West

FIGURE 42. Clemens with H. H. Rogers at the Princess Hotel, 1908 (courtesy the Mark Twain Project, the Bancroft Library).

Seventy-fifth Street, in New York. (She had not cast her net wide. Clemens played billiards with Irene in January, he said, and was amused to watch her seize advantage by freely repositioning the balls. He took to calling such a maneuver an "Irene.")

Now that he began to think of his gems of the first water as angelfish, Clemens compounded the metaphor by regarding his collection as a personal fish tank. "He has his aquarium of little girls," Miss Lyon wrote, "and they are all angelfish, while he wears a flying fish scarf pin, though he says he is a shad. Off he goes with a flash when he sees a new pair of slim little legs appear, and if the little girl wears butterfly bows of ribbon on the back of her head his delirium is complete." Miss Wallace was much kinder:

In this aquarium there were to be none but Angel-fish admitted. To be an Angel-fish one must be a girl, and one must be young, and one must have won Mr. Clemens's heart. This latter was not hard to do, for he always made the overtures when he first met, or saw, any promising candidate. . . .

The members of Mr. Clemens' aquarium felt for him the deep affection that children have for an older person who understands them and treats them with respect. He never talked down to them, but considered their opinions with proper dignity. . . .

This wonderful comprehension that he had of children, and his perfect sympathy for them, helped us to understand better the simplicity of his own character. When we were with him, we, too, felt like little children. All pretentious wisdom, all sophisticated phrases, all acquired and meaningless conventions were laid aside, and we said what we meant, and spontaneity took the place of calculation, and we became simple and unafraid, and sure of being understood.[5]

Clemens understood children so well because he never lost his boyhood, what he called the "dreamland of his life." Part of his plan in *The Adventures of Tom Sawyer*, he said in the preface, had been "to try to pleasantly remind adults of what they once were themselves, and of how they felt and thought and talked." Howells wrote that Clemens remained a youth until the end of his days, "the heart of a boy with the head of a sage."[6]

Once he found Irene—a beautiful and graceful and altogether wonderful child, he said—Clemens made another excursion to Spanish Point (FIG. 43). They rode in the cart, Reginald tended the donkey, and Miss Lyon, Miss Wallace, and Benjamin had to walk; only Rogers escaped from this slow, curious caravan. Two days later, on February 27, a ball game furnished their entertainment. Miss Lyon was happy to observe the next day how the two old friends gained strength. "The King drives out, and he walks out, and he is gay and young and full of a new and splendid life," she wrote. "Mr. Rogers is improving every day now, and he isn't the gray feeble man he was less than a week ago." When indoors, Clemens spent hours playing billiards with Irene and another child, Anne Fields, of Jersey City. That evening, before the regular Friday night hotel ball, his excellency the governor, Lt.-Gen. J. H. Wodehouse, arrived in regalia. Miss Lyon thought he looked like a parrot.

Rogers and Clemens often took short rides to town, and not without attracting notice. An idler on Front Street, the *Royal Gazette* reported, "may see almost

FIGURE 43. Irene Gerken with Clemens, 1908 (courtesy the Mark Twain Project, the Bancroft Library).

any afternoon, weather permitting, two quiet looking, white haired old gentlemen taking the air in an open carriage, chatting cosily and absorbing with shrewd glances from under bushy eyebrows the sights and the scenes of the street" (FIG. 44). Their reputations preceded them—perhaps with help from Upton Sinclair. The same piece said that Sinclair, a "representative of that fast growing class, the American Socialist," was currently rusticating in Somerset. Of the two old gentlemen that appeared on Front Street, the *Gazette* continued, one was known as a maker of merriment, while the other was "likewise in touch with the world but rather through their pockets than their sense of humour."[7] Miss Wallace maintained that Rogers, too, was a charming man "with a fund of quiet humor," but Clemens found that his association with Rogers prompted more questions than his public attentions to schoolgirls. When asked why he befriended a man of so much tainted money, he had a ready answer. "Yes," he said, "it's doubly tainted: t'aint yours, and t'aint mine."[8]

FIGURE 44. Front Street, Hamilton, 1899 (Coit album, the Bermuda Archives).

Another person who raised eyebrows, especially those of Miss Lyon and Miss Wallace, was the mysterious Mrs. Peck. At first, Miss Lyon simply recorded that she regularly wintered in Bermuda and called herself a "hardy annual." But soon she wrote that Mrs. Peck was "a bewitching woman, and a snare for men folk." People on the Islands, she added, "think she is not sincere." Miss Wallace, more reserved, reported that no husband was in sight, and "there was a little restless look of unfulfilment about her eyes and mouth that gave grounds for romantic speculation." They watched Mrs. Peck when she appeared at the hotel for tea on February 29 and conversed with a friend all the while in French. Clemens spent part of the day entertaining Irene. He gave her an inscribed copy of *Eve's Diary,* which he had lovingly written after the loss of his wife. That evening, lying on his bed and still wearing his white suit, he read aloud from the narrative poems of Kipling, who had just won the Nobel Prize. As he read *The "Mary Gloster,"* Miss Wallace and Miss Lyon broke into tears. Kipling himself once wrote of "the great and godlike Clemens," and said he had "the slowest, calmest, levellest voice in all the world" and spoke with a long, slow surge.[9] Other nights, Clemens repeated the performance in his room, where Mrs. Peck enjoyed the freedom to smoke. She finally asked him to read Kipling's poems for her guests at Shoreby, on March 27. "He read these in a tone and with a depth of feeling that gave to the verses a value seldom recognized," the *Royal Gazette* commented, perhaps with no irony intended.[10]

Miss Wallace had gone with her redoubtable mother—whom, annoyingly, she called "Lady Mother" throughout her memoir—and Margaret Blackmer to see the new island aquarium. It opened January 1 with a celebration that began when a steamer departed from the foot of Burnaby Street and proceeded west to Agar's Island, by Two Rock Passage (FIG. 45). Another excursion to the aquarium, on Sunday morning, March 1, was arranged for Clemens and his party by W. Maxwell Greene, the effervescent and obliging U.S. consul, as Miss Wallace described him. Goodwin Gosling, secretary to the Bermuda Natural History Society, also came aboard; he had urged the founding of a biological station and aquarium, a project that interested the presidents of Harvard, Princeton, and Columbia. Twelve fish tanks were cleverly constructed within a masonry moat around a powder magazine the Royal Navy had declared obsolete. Open to sunlight and fresh air, the tanks were designed to be approached through dark and mysterious chambers. "The fish were very wonderful in their coloring and form," Miss Wallace wrote, "but Mr. Clemens didn't seem to think that they were very sociable. And it *wasn't* very pleasant to see the octopus dine off a retiring and harmless crab."[11] Clemens, predictably, pronounced the blue and yellow angelfish his favorite. After a keeper prodded the octopus, so it was told, Clemens did the same to Rogers, and said, "There you are, H. H.—the Big Stick is after you, even down here."

As soon as the party got back to town, Miss Lyon reported, they "scrambled for cabs and drove up to Prospect to see the young soldiers and to hear the band." Prospect comprised high ground in Devonshire Parish, not far east of Hamilton, and accommodated the garrison of the regular army. The troops made a splendid show in their scarlet uniforms (FIG. 46). Tourists could attend Sunday services in the homely garrison chapel, a long narrow house, Miss Wallace noted in her journal, built of wood and covered with corrugated iron. The garrison maintained a school, theater, tennis courts, and playing fields. Sundays saw Clemens adopt a careful strategy. He would arrive too late for church but in time for the band, which played under a grove of cedars. On such outings he took further opportunities to poke fun of Rogers, calling him "the Rajah." At the hotel, he said Rogers entered the dining room as if he were the Gibbs Hill lighthouse, "stiff and tall, turning his lights from side to side." Clemens

FIGURE 45. Approach to Agar's Island aquarium (courtesy the New Jersey Historical Society).

FIGURE 46. Parade at Prospect, Devonshire Parish, about 1900 (courtesy the Bermuda Archives).

also persisted in saying "Bermooda," which Miss Wallace thought he had quaintly derived from Shakespeare's phrase, "the still-vex'd Bermoothes." Tom Moore, however, wrote that natives were saying "Bermooda" in 1804.

Clemens wrote Margaret Blackmer that he had returned to Spanish Point in the donkey cart with his new little friend, Irene Gerken. The same day, March 2, he wrote his daughter Jean that he was finding plenty of company at the Princess Hotel, where dances were held two nights a week. "The roads are good & we drive a deal; when we are not driving we still live out-doors in the sun & gather health," he wrote. "The hotels are full—and more than full. The cottages are full also. The weekly steamer brought 255 people this morning, & they are around skirmishing for shelter." Teams from the two large hotels played a baseball game on Wednesday, and Clemens could be seen through "a cloud of smoke which rolled from a big, black cigar." He cheered for the Princess team, but it lost.[12]

At long last, Bermuda enjoyed Mark Twain on stage. It was a dream come true, said the *Royal Gazette*. Advertised as an "entertainment" to benefit the Cottage Hospital, the event was held on Thursday, March 5, in the Princess ballroom. Admittance cost two shillings. Mark Twain was master of ceremonies. After performances by several amateur musicians and an impersonator of vaudeville characters, he said that meeting General Miles at a party in New York had reminded him of the life he led in Washington, D.C., more than forty years earlier. He was rooming with another newspaper correspondent, and they had to live on twenty-four dollars a week. His friend was a Scotch Presbyterian, a "Presbyterian of the old and genuine school, being honest and sincere in his religion and loving it," but still burdened by "a large and grateful sympathy with Scotch whisky." Mark Twain now warmed to his story of the three-dollar dog, a tale he had told best in a dictation on October 3, 1907:

In some ways I was always honest; even from my earliest years I could never bring myself to use money which I had acquired in questionable ways; many a time I tried, but principle was always stronger than desire. . . .

I remember a time when a shortage occurred; we had to have three dollars, and we had to have it before the close of the day. I don't know now how we happened to want all that money at one time; I only know we had to have it. Swinton told me to go out and find it, and he said he would also go out and see what he could do. He didn't seem to have any doubt that we would succeed, but I knew that that was his religion working in him; I hadn't the same confidence; I hadn't any idea where to turn to raise all that bullion and I said so. I think he was ashamed of me, privately, because of my weak faith. He told me to give myself no uneasiness, no concern; & said in a simple, confident, & unquestioning way, "the Lord will provide." I saw that he fully believed the Lord would provide, but it seemed to me that if he had had my experience—

But never mind that; before he was done with me his strong faith had had its influence, and I went forth from the place almost convinced that the Lord really would provide.

I wandered around the streets for an hour, trying to think up some way to get that money, but nothing suggested itself. At last I lounged into the big lobby of the Ebbitt House, which was then a new hotel, and sat down. Presently a dog came loafing along. He paused, glanced up at me and said with his eyes, "Are you friendly?" I answered with my eyes that I was. He gave his tail a grateful little wag and came forward and rested his jaw on my knee and lifted his brown eyes to my face in a winningly affectionate way. He was a lovely creature, as beautiful as a girl, and he was made all of silk & velvet. I stroked his smooth brown head and fondled his drooping ears, and we were a pair of lovers right away. Pretty soon Brig.-General Miles, the hero of the land, came strolling by in his blue and gold splendors with everybody's admiring gaze upon him. He saw the dog and stopped, and there was a light in his eye which showed that he had a warm place in his heart for dogs like this gracious creature; then he came forward and patted the dog and said,

"He is very fine—he is a wonder; would you sell him?"

I was greatly moved; it seemed a marvelous thing to me, the way Swinton's prediction had come true. I said,

"Yes."

The General said, "What do you ask for him?"

"Three dollars."

The General was manifestly surprised. He said, "Three dollars? Only three dollars? Why that dog is a most uncommon dog; he can't possibly be worth less than fifty. If he were mine, I wouldn't take a hundred for him. I'm afraid you are not aware of his value. Reconsider your price if you like, I don't wish to wrong you."

But if he had known me he would have known that I was no more capable of wronging him than he was of wronging me. I responded with the same quiet decision as before,

"No, three dollars. That is his price."

"Very well, since you insist upon it," said the General, and he gave me three dollars and led the dog away, and disappeared upstairs.

In about ten minutes a gentle-faced middle-aged gentleman came along, and began to look around here and there and under tables and everywhere, and I said to him,

"Is it a dog you are looking for?"

His face had been sad, before, and troubled; but it lit up gladly now, and he answered,

"Yes—have you seen him?"

"Yes," I said, "he was here a minute ago, and I saw him follow a gentleman away. I think I could find him for you if you would like me to try."

I have seldom seen a person look so grateful—and there was gratitude in his voice, too, when he conceded that he would like me to try. I said I would do it with great pleasure but that as it might take a little time I hoped he would not mind paying me something for my trouble. He said he would do it most gladly—repeating that phrase "most gladly"—and asked me how much. I said—

"Three dollars."

He looked surprised, and said,

"Dear me, it is nothing! I will pay you ten, quite willingly."

But I said, "No, three is the price," and I started for the stairs without waiting for any further argument, for Swinton had said that that was the amount that the Lord would provide and it seemed to me that it would be sacrilegious to take a penny more than was promised.

I got the number of the General's room from the office-clerk, as I passed by his wicket, and when I reached the room I found the General there caressing his dog, and quite happy. I said,

"I am sorry, but I have to take the dog again."

He seemed very much surprised, and said, "Take him again? Why, he is my dog; you sold him to me, and at your own price."

"Yes," I said, "it is true—but I have to have him, because the man wants him again."

"What man?"

"The man that owns him; he wasn't my dog."

The General looked even more surprised than before, and for a moment he couldn't seem to find his voice; then he said, "Do you mean to tell me that you were selling another man's dog—and knew it?"

"Yes, I knew it wasn't my dog."

"Then why did you sell him?"

I said,

"Well, that is a curious question to ask. I sold him because you wanted him. You offered to buy the dog; you can't deny that. I was not anxious to sell him—I had not even thought of selling him—but it seemed to me that if it could be any accommodation to you—"

He broke me off in the middle, and said,

"*Accommodation* to me? It is the most extraordinary spirit of accommodation I have ever heard of—the idea of your selling a dog that didn't belong to you—"

I broke him off there and said, "There is no relevancy about this kind of argument; you said yourself that the dog was probably worth a hundred dollars. I only asked you three; was there anything unfair about that? You offered to pay more, you know you did. I only asked you three; you can't deny it."

"Oh, what in the world has that to do with it! The crux of the matter is that you didn't own the dog—can't you see that? You seem to think that there is no impropriety in selling property that isn't yours provided you sell it cheap. Now, then—"

I said, "Please don't argue about it anymore. You can't get around the fact that the price was perfectly fair, perfectly reasonable—considering that I didn't own the dog—and so arguing about it is only a waste of words. I have to have him back again because the man wants him; don't you see that I haven't any choice in the matter? Put yourself in my place. Suppose you had sold a dog that didn't belong to you; suppose you—"

"Oh," he said, "don't muddle my brains any more with your idiotic reasonings! Take him along, and give me a rest."

So I paid back the three dollars and led the dog downstairs and passed him over to his owner, and collected three for my trouble.

I went away with a good conscience, because I had acted honorably; I never could have used the three that I sold the dog for, because it was not rightly my own, but the three I got for restoring him to his rightful owner was righteously and properly mine, because I had earned it. That man might never have gotten the dog back at all, if it hadn't been for me. My principles have remained to this day what they were then. I was always honest; I know I can never be otherwise. . . .

Now, then, that is the tale. Some of it is true.

Mark Twain told the story as though for the first time, aiming for what he defined in his autobiography as "the captivating naturalness of an impromptu narration." He added an "application," another of his techniques. "My friend was partly right," he said, "when he assured me that the 'Lord would provide,' but it is really rather doubtful whether the Lord really would have provided for us if I had not bestirred myself." He continued:

The Bermuda Hospital needs financial assistance and it is very easy and very pleasant to believe that the Lord will provide for such a worthy institution, but it is safer for us to bestir ourselves a little. . . . Therefore, give generously tonight to the cause. The larger the sums, the more cordially they will be received, and if you have not brought your purses with you, the ladies may contribute their jewels and the gentlemen their letters of credit, or express checks, properly endorsed. This does not mean that small sums will not be politely received, but simply means that the degree of enthusiasm for a shilling may be slightly less than for one hundred pounds. . . . And in closing, Ladies and Gentlemen, let me remind you that the hospital is always fighting pain, and pain is a King who is no respecter of persons.[13]

The parlors of the Princess Hotel, said Miss Wallace, were packed that night to suffocation. Mark Twain wrote some years earlier that "the welcome which an American lecturer gets from a British colonial audience is a thing which will move him to his deepest deeps, and veil his sight and break his voice." At one point in telling the story he broke into boyish laughter. It was a rare violation of his platform style, Rogers recognized immediately. ("The humorous story," Mark Twain wrote, "is told gravely; the teller does his best to conceal the fact that he even dimly suspects that there is anything funny about it.")[14]

The performance must have tired him. At billiards the next day, Miss Lyon recorded, a German visitor was taking his photograph when Clemens got a sudden "crick in his neck." She watched through a window onto the porch and saw him "pale as death, leaning over the table, and the young German rubbing the back of his head." Later that day he set out for Spanish Point but failed to get there.

One day, he got an unusually polite luncheon invitation from John Gay, the chaplain aboard HMS *Cressy*, and H. W. Finlayson, the fleet surgeon. Although he could claim to be only a "very unworthy collateral descendant of the poet," Gay wrote, he and Clemens in fact were first cousins. Clemens boarded the admiral's launch to be conveyed to the *Cressy*, one of three warships anchored at the Dockyard (FIG. 47). He took along William E. Benjamin—"the brightest man in these regions," he said, "& the best company." It was Tuesday, March 10, and the excursion made a perfect day. Clemens wrote Dorothy Quick that he had a "screaming good time" telling stories at the officers' mess.[15]

Dorothy had written that she was sick again, but hoped Clemens was enjoying the lilies and sunshine in Bermuda. "I *know* you ought to come here," he answered on March 10:

This heavenly climate & fine air would soon make you strong & well. . . . [Y]ou need to get away from doctors & let generous & wise Nature build you up & make you strong. Come to me, you dear Dorothy! You will be so welcome.

FIGURE 47. Dockyard, Ireland Island, Sandys Parish.

Miss Lyon is getting strong & robust, & Mr. Rogers is improving so decidedly that he has stopped talking about going back home—so I am hoping & expecting to keep him here until April 11.

We are having very lively times every day—sailing, driving, walking, lunching, dancing; & at night we play billiards & cards & never go out, to dinners or anywhere else. I am now so strong that I suppose I could pull up one of these islands by the roots & throw it half way to New York. In fact I know I could.

On March 12 he wrote Dorothy again, and told her he had attended a garden party the day before at Government House, the palatial residence of the Crown's representative. Clemens continued:

Today, five of us men drove to St. George's, over beautiful roads with charming scenery & the wonderful blue water always in sight—distance 12 miles—& we dined at the hotel. However, on the way there we visited a wonderful cave that was discovered in December by a couple of black boys—the most beautiful cave in the world, I suppose. We descended 150 steps & stood in a splendid place 250 feet long & 30 or 40 wide, with a brilliant lake of clear water under our feet & all the roof overhead splendid with shining stalactites, thousands & thousands of them as white as sugar, & thousands & thousands brown & pink & other tints. All lighted with acetylene jets.[16]

Clemens still took pleasure along the roads he traveled in 1877 or even earlier, and found enchantment in the Crystal Cave, discovered on the Wilkinson estate not far from Walsingham (FIG. 48). The cave and the aquarium, with what he believed "the most beautiful fish that swims," were the two new tourist attractions of 1908. The sight again of slowly dripping water could take Clemens all the way back to Hannibal, and to McDowell's Cave, which became the haunting "McDougal's Cave" in *The Adventures of Tom Sawyer*. ("That drop was falling when the Pyramids were new; when Troy fell; when the foundations of Rome were laid; when Christ was crucified; when the Conquerer created the British empire; when Columbus sailed; when the massacre at Lexington was 'news.'") The *Royal Gazette* had described the Crystal Cave on January 11 as having been discovered "twelve months or so ago." Later, however, Albert Bigelow

FIGURE 48. Crystal Cave and Cahow Lake, Hamilton Parish.

Paine learned that it was found in March 1905 by a boy named Carl Gibbon, then fourteen. As he rested in the sun with Edgar Hollis, his friend, Carl felt a cool current of air issuing from a crevice in the hillside. The boys dug a larger opening and daringly penetrated the cave. Almost a year later, in February 1906, Louis L. Mowbray, the young but already distinguished naturalist, came upon a petrel of unknown species in a rocky nest on Castle Island. When he and Goodwin Gosling went into the Crystal Cave and descended to a pool, they matched the bird from Castle Island with fossilized bones and embedded feathers, and thereby identified it as the long-lost but periodically rediscovered Bermuda petrel (*Pterodroma cahow*). Hence the underground pool was named Cahow Lake. These peculiar birds were thought to have been extinguished at the beginning of the seventeenth century by hungry castaways and the early settlers. Capt. Diego Ramirez wrote of a night in 1603 when his shipwrecked crew on Spanish Point encountered the nocturnal, shrieking cahows: "More than 500 birds were brought off to the ship that night, and, having gone through hot water and been plucked, proved to be very fat and fine. Thereafter a capture was made every evening. The birds were so plentiful that 4,000 could be taken in a single bag. The men relished them enough to eat them all the time, and when we left we brought away more than 1,000 well dried and salted for the voyage."[17]

Apart from touring, Clemens continued to stock his personal aquarium. Miss Wallace observed his technique, then wrote in her journal: "If a child of ten or twelve happens to be anywhere within the radius of his glance, he is inevitably sure of seeing her. Then begins the most delightful flirtation. The King nods— if that is not effective he beckons with his hand and sometimes he goes up to the child and makes a remark that seems to continue a conversation broken off at some remoter period. He is nearly always sure to win their hearts." Clemens quickly caught two more angelfish, Helen Martin, a twelve year old from Montreal, and Jean Spurr, thirteen, of Newark, New Jersey. Jean wore a blonde wig and had no eyebrows or lashes, Miss Lyon wrote, but the King overlooked such attributes. "He sees into her fair young soul," she ventured. Nor did it bother the King that newspapers regularly took note of his young girlfriends. Later, when the *Bermudian* carried Jean Spurr back to New York, she proudly displayed Mark Twain's autograph on a hotel dance program. She had told him the room looked crowded with old maids, and he responded by inscribing one of his epigrams from *Pudd'nhead Wilson:* "Consider well the proportions of things. It is better to be a young June-bug than an old bird of paradise."[18] And in a belated report on "Mark Twain's Outing in Bermuda," the *New York Times* published a photograph of Clemens standing on a dock with Irene Gerken, who had left the Islands on March 10.[19]

On March 15, after another Sunday morning drive to Prospect for the band concert, Clemens and his party rode to Shoreby, where Mrs. Peck entertained them with her favorite dish, West Indian pepper pot. It was brought to the table in a "big black heavy old kettle," Miss Lyon said. Typically, pepper pot took three or four days to prepare, with strips of pork, beef, and poultry cooked with cassareep, peppers, thyme, and salt.[20] Mrs. Peck said it was a heathen dish, best enjoyed on Sundays. Although mild at first taste, Miss Wallace wrote, it soon began to burn insidiously. Clemens approved, but said a little more pepper was needed. The day ended in his hotel room with more readings from Kipling's poems.

Emilie Rogers, the Rajah's wife, arrived in Bermuda the next day. She, too, was in poor health. Mrs. Rogers had endeared herself to Clemens in the fall of 1906 by giving him a billiard table for his Fifth Avenue home. Paine was grateful because it was over billiards, he said, that Clemens became his friend and not simply the subject of his monumental biography. The climate of the Islands seemed not to agree with Mrs. Rogers, even though Clemens had written Francesca that the weather was perfect and the days were like those New York might see in June. Before the week was over she nevertheless organized a party of eleven for an excursion to Somerset. Two days later, on March 23, Clemens ventured on a long picnic with Jean Spurr and Helen Martin. That night he wrote his daughter Clara:

> We are having good times. To-day I went pic-nicking with some other children, & romped in the sand on the sea-shore about 6 hours. I returned dog-tired, & at first I thought I oughtn't to have went, but 2 hours of billiards rested me up again.
>
> Mr. Rogers was pretty poorly when we came down here, & Miss Lyon was not much better off. But both are in much improved condition now. There was nothing the matter with me, yet I seem to have improved a little myself.

Miss Wallace and her Lady Mother sailed from Bermuda the next day, Tuesday. They missed hearing more band concerts at Prospect and more poems of Kipling's. At the concert on Sunday, March 29, Miss Lyon watched Clemens quietly

sitting apart from the "feminine chatter" so he could enjoy the music. In the afternoon he went swimming on the South Shore. "The King at 72 was as young
and vigorous in his wide strokes as a youth would have been," she wrote. He went
boating on Monday. Two distinguished persons were among the passengers who
arrived on the *Bermudian* that morning: the fourth Earl Grey, governor-general
of Canada, who was escorted to Government House with great fanfare, and
Nicholas Murray Butler, president of Columbia University. Both joined Clemens
the next day for another sail. Back at the hotel, the King spied another potential
angelfish. Her name was Helen S. Allen. Not a tourist, she had come to watch
the dancing. Helen was thirteen. Clemens asked her to join him, and repeated
the gesture the following night. She invited him to her home the next day.
Helen lived just across Pitt's Bay from the hotel, at the far side of Cockle Point
(FIG. 49). It was an easy walk to her home, an old place named Bay House
(FIG. 50).

In a coincidence worthy of Dickens, she had been born at Wistowe and was
the granddaughter of Charles M. Allen, the war consul appointed by President
Lincoln. "Mr. Clemens had known Helen's grandfather when he was American
consul, in the days of *Innocents Abroad,*" wrote Helen's mother, Marion Schuyler
Allen, in several different typescript versions of a memoir.[21] Helen's grandmother
knew Clemens's wife when Livy was only a small child. As soon as Clemens
heard about Helen's family, he visited Grandmother Allen at the family home in
Flatts. They talked for an hour and a half about the Langdon family and friends
in Elmira, New York. Clemens discovered her just in time. Susan Elizabeth Allen
was eighty-two, and died the next year. Helen's father, William H. Allen, served
under Maxwell Greene as the American vice-consul. Clemens found the Allen
family to be exceptionally hospitable, and began saying that Abraham Lincoln
had brought them all together. On his final voyages to Bermuda he made Bay
House his home.

Helen and her mother persuaded him to attend a children's party aboard
HMS *Euryalus,* the flagship of the North America and West Indies station, on
Saturday afternoon, April 4. Sailors costumed as pirates staged a capture of the
ship, and two officers walked the plank. Clemens ate cake (fourteen different
kinds were served), wrote Miss Lyon, drank ginger beer, and adorned Helen
with his Panama hat. Sunday, he went back to Prospect to watch a regimental
parade with Lord Grey, "a winning and loveable man and a fine and sterling character," Clemens said in dictating more of his autobiography eleven days later.

By now his entertainments had become repetitive, perhaps even tiresome. A

FIGURE 49. Cockle Point, Pembroke Parish.

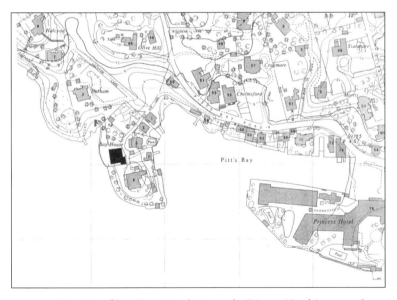

FIGURE 50. Location of Bay House in relation to the Princess Hotel (courtesy the Ministry of Works & Engineering, Hamilton).

sturdy Presbyterian conscience might frown upon frivolous retirement at any age. "I have led a lazy & comfortable life here for six weeks," Clemens wrote to Clara. "It is a most pleasant & useless life,—as far as other people are concerned. I have been useful only once. I talked for the hospital one night, & made some money for it. Next Thursday [April 9] I am to be useful again—a talk for the aquarium, which is the governor's pet, & a very worthy one. It will be a great institution by & by." Clemens had been reading *The Mother of the Man,* a new book by Eden Phillpotts, whom he had met in London in 1900. He wrote Phillpotts a few weeks later that he had read and reread the book with high admiration. "I wish I had energy enough to resume work upon one or two of my several half-finished books," Clemens said, "but that is a dream, & won't ever come true."

The next morning, April 6, Clemens returned to Prospect and reported to the garrison school, where he had been asked to speak. First, the pupils sang old English hymns. The songs brought him to tears. Then, with the gravity and measured cadences that characterized his platform technique, he began to talk about cats:

As I was on my way up the hill, I saw a cat jump over a wall, and that reminded me of a little incident of my childhood that may interest you. I was a little boy once on a time, and before that I was a little girl, perhaps, though I don't remember it.

There was a good deal of cholera around the Mississippi Valley in those days, and my mother used to dose us children with a medicine called Patterson's Patent Pain Killer. She had an idea that the cholera was worse than the medicine, but then she had never taken the stuff. It went down our insides like liquid fire and fairly doubled us up. I suppose we took fifty bottles of that pain killer in our family. I used to feed mine to a crack in the floor of our room when no one was looking.

One day when I was doing this our cat, whose name was Peter, came into the room, and I looked at him and wondered if he might not like some of that pain killer. He looked hungry, and it seemed to me that a little of it might do him good. So I just poured out the bottle and put it before him. He did not seem to get the real effect of it at first, but pretty soon I saw him turn and look at me with a queer expression in his eyes, and the next minute he jumped to the window and went through it like a cyclone, taking all the flower pots with him; and seeing that cat on the wall just now reminded me of the little incident of my childhood after many years.

He had told the story of Peter the cat and the painkiller more than thirty years earlier, in *The Adventures of Tom Sawyer*.[22] The children broke into laughter and gave Clemens four great cheers as he was about to leave. That afternoon he took tea at the Arts and Crafts Association on Reid Street.

Some weeks earlier, Clemens had sailed to the coral reefs with Zoheth S. Freeman, his banker and friend, who was vacationing in Bermuda with his family, and with Rogers, Miss Lyon, and others. Miss Wallace said he could not be persuaded into a large glass-bottom boat for viewing the Sea Gardens, advertised as "a submarine realm of enchantment." His excuse was that he had already seen coral reefs at Nassau. But he returned to the Sea Gardens on Tuesday, April 7, with Rogers, Lord Grey, and the governor and his wife. He looked at the fish, the coral, the sea fans, and sponges. Deeper spots seemed to him like scenes of sagebrush and the desert, landscapes familiar from the years of *Roughing It*. Later, the group rode east to Tucker's Town, at Castle Harbor. They returned through Flatts and took tea at an old double house named Frascati, which had been made into a hotel.

The excursion party on Thursday morning numbered fifteen persons. They headed to St. George's for lunch. At table, Clemens was not feeling well, and he returned to the Princess Hotel. He wanted to rest for the last stage appearance he would make on the Islands. The event that night was a benefit for the Agar's Island aquarium. It was held in the Colonial Opera House, on Victoria Street. "Who would not wish the Biological Station to be in a chronic state of indigence," the *Royal Gazette* commented, "if measures for affording it relief involved on each occasion the appearance in public of the prince of American humorists?"[23] In dictating more of his autobiography on April 16, Clemens noted that because the Colonial Opera House had no stage door, he was escorted down the central aisle to the front row. He was seated next to a man he failed to recognize as H. C. Gollan, the chief justice, who was waiting to introduce him to the audience. At last, the orchestra struck up "God Save the King" for the entrance of the governor and his wife, and Lord Grey and Countess Grey. Clemens said Providence interfered to save him ("the first favor I have received from that source this year") just as he was about to mutter, "Now if the damned Chief Justice would arrive and do his stunt the show could proceed."

Mark Twain's topic was titled "Caprices of Memory," a routine catchall for a collection of tales not inherently related, with the exception of those about watermelons. Watermelons were a favorite theme. "The true Southern water-melon," he wrote in *Pudd'nhead Wilson,* "is a boon apart, and not to be mentioned with commoner things. It is chief of this world's luxuries, king by the grace of God over all the fruits of the earth."[24] In that spirit, he told his best stories of the evening:

I remember now as if it were yesterday the first time I ever stole a water-melon. I think it was the first time. I stole that watermelon out of a farmer's wagon while he was waiting on another customer. I carried it out to the seclusion of the lumberyard and broke it open. It was green. The greenest watermelon that was ever raised in the Mississippi Valley. When I saw it was green I was sorry and I began to reflect. Seemed to me I had done wrong.

I thought, "Now, what ought a boy to do? What ought a right-thinking, clean-hearted, high-principled boy to do who has stolen a green water-melon? What would George Washington do?"

I said to myself, "There is only one thing for him to do. He must restore that stolen watermelon."

Not many boys would do that. I did. I rose up spiritually strengthened and refreshed and I carried it back and restored it to the farmer—what was left of it. And I made him give me a ripe one.

I was severe with him. I told him he ought to be ashamed of himself going around working off green watermelons on people who had confidence in him. I told him if he did not break himself of that habit he would not have any more of my custom.

He said it would not happen again, and I know it was a lesson to that man, and it was such a pleasure to me to reflect that perhaps I saved that man, set him on the right path with his face pointing toward ultimate righteousness.

Now, that was sufficient reward for me, and I got a watermelon besides. That is the way moral character is built up—by personal experience. . . . I have never stolen a watermelon of that character since. . . .

I was kept at home one day. I was thirteen or fourteen years old. It was one Saturday afternoon and I was kept at home because of one of those experiments of mine in moral philosophy. I did have one little satisfaction. I had half a watermelon. I dug it out until only the shell remained and it formed a sort of canoe. It seemed a pity to waste that. I didn't know what to do with it.

I thought at last I would drop it on somebody's head. Three-story window. Every temptation. I watched people come along down below in order to pick out the right person. It is possible to drop a watermelon on the wrong man's head.

At last my younger brother came along. When I saw him I knew that he was delivered into my hands. I never took more interest in any work of art in the world than I did in measuring his distance from me, and his rate of progress. I held that canoe out of the window over his head. I could see him foreshorten until his nose and toes were on a line.

When I judged he was six feet from the point where the melon would land I released it. It was beautiful to see the operation of that exact calculation I made. It hit him right on top of the head. There was an explosion. The shell burst into a thousand pieces and chunks of it broke windows three miles around.

That taught me I was born for the military service. I joined the military forces at the beginning of the Civil War. I served a couple of weeks.[25]

He was thanked by Governor Wodehouse, who said Bermuda hoped to see him again next year, and in full health and strength. Clemens must have looked less than robust, but he did his best to appear otherwise. Friday, when he went back to Bay House for a swim with Helen Allen, he struck a sturdy pose (FIG. 51).

The long Bermuda holiday was over. Clemens and his group joined Lord Grey in boarding the *Bermudian* on Saturday, April 11. The ship was also carrying sixty thousand Easter lilies for Sunday, April 19, and a few Bermuda angelfish for the aquarium in Battery Park. It docked in New York on Monday. "I offered to loan Rogers $2," Clemens told the newspapermen, "though I knew I was taking an awful risk. Rogers thought it was simply a courtesy and so did not take me up. Now I am $2 ahead." He told of stormy seas, and standing in his white suit at the stern rail with Dorothy Sturgis, a sixteen year old from Boston whom he appointed a new angelfish. The ocean became most rude, he said, and they got drenched by a giant wave.[26]

FIGURE 51. Clemens with Helen Allen at Bay House, April 1908 (courtesy the Mark Twain Project, the Bancroft Library).

A few days later he composed a letter to his angelfish in Montreal:

> I miss you, dear Helen. I miss Bermuda, too, but not so much as I miss you; for you were rare, & occasional, & select, & Ltd., whereas Bermuda's charms & graciousness were free & common & unrestricted,—like the rain, you know, which falls upon the just & unjust alike; a thing which would not happen if I were superintending the rain's affairs. No, I would rain softly & sweetly upon the just, but whenever I caught a sample of the unjust out-doors I would drown him.[27]

Later that month, Clemens rode with Dorothy Quick, Miss Lyon, and Ashcroft to the aquarium in Battery Park. The freshly imported angelfish had already died. They talked about his long holiday on the Islands. "If an American died and went to Bermuda," Clemens said to Dorothy, "he would think he's arrived in Heaven."[28]

VII

ON DOCTOR'S ORDERS, 1909

Miss Lyon kept a close eye on Clemens, his behavior and health. When he spoke on behalf of the children's theater of the Educational Alliance, on April 23, 1908, she saw he was not himself. "He miscalled words, and seemed to have great difficulty in holding his thoughts together," she wrote, "but I was the only one who knew it." A few days later, Andrew Carnegie sent him another supply of Scotch. "The whisky came at the right time," Clemens wrote him. "Of course—for whisky never comes at the wrong time." He appended a poem of Byron's, and altered the last line. The verses were jovial but slightly ominous:

> My boat is by the shore
> And my bark is on the sea,
> But before I go, Tom Moore,
> Here's a health to Carnegie.

Clemens was preparing to move to rural Connecticut. His desire to own a summer place had been prompted by Albert Bigelow Paine, who bought an old house near Redding in the fall of 1905. It was only two hours by train from New York. The next year, Clemens began to accumulate acreage next to Paine's small property. Strangely, he never troubled to visit the site. In the summer of 1906 he commissioned John Mead Howells, his old friend's son, to design a residence. (In a later year, Howells teamed with Raymond Hood and won the international competition for a tower to house the *Chicago Tribune*.) Miss Lyon thought the country house should be named "Autobiography House," because most of its cost would be met by the thirty thousand dollars that George Harvey generously paid for the series of twenty-five installments of Mark Twain's autobiography he was publishing in the *North American Review*. But she was surprised to see the King so royally disengaged from the project. "Mr. Clemens refuses to discuss the subject," she noted on April 9, 1907. "He won't allow himself to be informed or consulted. . . . He doesn't want to see it, or hear anything about it. He leaves all the affairs now with John Howells and me."

Clemens said later that he deliberately entrusted the house to his architect, his daughter Clara, and Miss Lyon:

> I had every confidence in their taste and judgment and none in my own. My meddling would only have made confusion. I was not willing to discuss the plans nor look at the drawings. I merely said I wanted three things—a room of my own that would be quiet, a billiard-room big enough to play in without jabbing the cues into the wall, and a living-room forty by twenty feet. For the rest they could do as they liked, and I had nothing more to do with the house. . . . I didn't want any of the bother of building.[1]

As it turned out, the part of the house Clemens valued most highly was the loggia. Howells had graduated from Harvard and the École des Beaux Arts in Paris. He knew Clemens had spent many years abroad and was accustomed, wherever he might be living, to spending time on verandas or porches. Howells conceived a stately mansion in the spirit of an Italian villa. Having built and furnished the house sight unseen, Clemens arrived in Redding on June 18, 1908. He had expressed doubts about a site that seemed too distant; he worried that he might be left alone, without his daughters. But he quickly settled in, and made it his year-round home (FIG. 52). "I realize that this is the most satisfactory house I was ever in, & also the most beautiful," he wrote Clara on June 20. "The Hartford house was a lovely home, but the architect damaged many of its comfort-possibilities & wasted a deal of its space. The New York house is a roomy & pleasant house, but it is sunless, not beautiful."

Yet the villa near Redding was too large for such a lonely man. Clemens kept servants, and Miss Lyon and Ashcroft and Paine were around, but not always. It was an odd household at its happiest, and it would decline into a stifling realm

FIGURE 52. At Stormfield, 1908 (courtesy the Mark Twain Project, the Bancroft Library).

of intrigue and alienation.[2] Clemens deemed his friendships with schoolgirls much more pure and dependable. He made the new billiard room the head-quarters for his aquarium, and decorated the walls with portraits of the girls and pictures of various fish. He also admitted two more angelfish: Louise Paine, the eldest daughter of his biographer, and Dorothy Harvey, the daughter of his pub-lisher (FIG. 53). "My house is named 'Innocence at Home,'" he wrote Margaret Blackmer on July 7, "& it is the angel-fishes that are to furnish the innocence, though the public don't know that. It isn't the public's affair." Clara Clemens disapproved of the name "Innocence at Home," now printed on her father's sta-tionery, and she urged him to change it. Much later, when Paine had occasion to write Helen Allen's mother, he told her Clara "never quite liked her father's at-tentions to young girls (or old ones either, for that matter) in public." Mrs. Allen also received a letter directly from Clara, who warned that anything Clemens wrote to little girls should be considered insignificant and purely personal, and ought

FIGURE 53. In the aquarium with Louise Paine and Dorothy Harvey, 1908 (courtesy the Mark Twain Project, the Bancroft Library).

not to be published. Eventually, the house got a different name. "Stormfield" was better, Clemens wrote his daughter Jean, because the house stood on high ground and was exposed to storms, and the loggia (with the suite of rooms above it, for Clara) had been built from his sale of "Extract from Captain Stormfield's Visit to Heaven," an old story he revived and published in two issues of *Harper's Monthly.*[3] But he wrote that Stormfield would be only the public name, and Innocence at Home would continue to serve for the headquarters of his aquarium.

Late in July 1908, Clemens grew dizzy at the billiard table and suffered a temporary loss of memory. Paine realized only later that it was the first sign of the King's serious illness. Clemens became sick ten days later, and had been much depressed by the sudden death on August 1 of his talented nephew, Samuel Moffett, an editor at *Collier's.* "I have retired from New York for good," he wrote Howells on August 12. "I have retired from labor for good. I have dismissed my stenographer & have entered upon a holiday whose other end is in the cemetery." Paine told Miss Lyon that the King's billiard game was slipping. She was also advised by George Harvey that the cold and lonely days of an early winter in the country would make him gloomy. Friends should be regularly invited to Stormfield, the colonel said. Margaret Blackmer and Francesca visited, and so did Laura Hawkins Frazer, whom Clemens called his very first sweetheart; she had furnished the model for Becky Thatcher in *The Adventures of Tom Sawyer*. Miss Wallace, ever devoted, arrived at the Redding station on Thanksgiving Day. Riding toward the King's residence, she noticed little road signs initialed "M. T." She came prepared to keep a record of her visit. Later, she wrote of Stormfield:

> It was singularly in keeping with the dark, straight cedars which nature had foreseeingly disposed in decorative lines and groups. Inside there was spaciousness, light, perfect comfort, and simplicity; while outside there was all the beauty of a New England landscape at its best, with nothing abrupt or harsh in the undulating curves of its hills and valleys; with something maternal in its soft, full outlines—where it would seem a sweet and restful thing to lay one's tired body down and let this mother Earth soothe and enfold you.[4]

Miss Wallace brought a second journal, still blank. "Stormfield. Nov. 28, 1908," Clemens wrote on the first page. "Betsy hasn't written in this book yet, but she's going to. It's to be called *Betsy's Heavenly Experiences at Stormfield*. She is certainly an angel" (FIG. 54). He gave her a copy of *Eve's Diary* before she left. It was the last time they saw each other.

The public would soon learn all about the new house, its beauty and the glory of its site. Neltje DeGraff Doubleday was at work on a fine article about the King and Stormfield for the April 1909 number of *Country Life in America*, a magazine published by the company Frank Doubleday, her husband, had founded. Just before Christmas, the remarkable American photographer Alvin Langdon Coburn arrived in Redding with Archibald Henderson, who had introduced Clemens to George Bernard Shaw. Coburn took a series of portraits to illustrate Henderson's forthcoming biography of Mark Twain. First, however, they collaborated on an article for the May 1909 number of *Harper's Monthly*. The same issue carried a piece by Paine titled "Mark Twain at Stormfield." Paine knew better, but his account was full of sweetness and light and cheer over the King's good health:

> He is seventy-three, but he is not old, and he never will be. He could not be old if he tried. His manner, his speech, his movement, his point of

FIGURE 54. Elizabeth Wallace at Stormfield, November 1908 (courtesy the Mark Twain Project, the Bancroft Library).

view—they are all young. His complexion is of exquisite coloring; he runs lightly up-stairs; he skips like a lad of ten. One never feels that he is old—that he ever could be old. His hair is snow-white, but then so is his dress, and there is as much of freshness and youth and joy in the one as in the other. He is the embodiment of eternal youth, with youth's eternal charm."[5]

Clemens suffered over the years from rheumatism in his writing arm, and from gout, lumbago, and chronic bronchitis. He still had his incomparable sense of humor, and still knew how to think, a rare distinction at any age. But he smoked all the time, drank whisky, ate very little, and sometimes flew into rages. Once again he was saddened by a death, that of his dear friend H. H. Rogers on May 19, 1909. Early in June, a few days before he was to speak to Francesca's graduating class at St. Timothy's School, in Maryland, he was stricken by his first severe chest pains from heart disease. Clemens proceeded to give the talk. It was to be his last public speech. Francesca by now was eighteen, and in July he wrote her candidly about the diagnosis. He said he was compelled to spend most of his time in his room and usually in bed, and was now smoking only four times a day instead of forty. "As a rule," he wrote, "the pains come only about twice a day; & the rest of the day is comfortable, & also agreeable. Idleness is my occupation; life is become a continuous holiday; a pleasant one, too, on the whole." Clemens stayed at Stormfield. He began to ponder how long it took to-bacco to damage his heart. Sixty-three years, he calculated. When he was twenty-five, a fortune-teller in New Orleans said she could almost promise he would live to be eighty-six if only he were to give up tobacco.[6]

As his chest pains continued, Bermuda grew more distant. "I am a prisoner in the house these past 3 months," he wrote September 10 on a postcard to Helen Allen, "& am not likely to get out for a year or so. If I were well enough I would take a run to Bermuda." Eleven days later he wrote her again. "I am not likely to see New York or Bermuda for a long long time," he said. "I don't go out of the house." In mid-October, Helen and her mother spent a night at Stormfield, where Clara Clemens and the pianist Ossip Gabrilowitsch had been married on October 6. They met Jean Clemens and the butler, Claude Benchotte, and they would see more of Claude the next year in Bermuda. "She has grown consider-ably," Clemens said of Helen when he wrote Miss Wallace on November 10, "but is as sweet & innocent & unspoiled a child as ever she was." He had been working on *Letters from the Earth,* a devastating critique of Christian doctrine and virtually a companion to Nietzsche's *Genealogy of Morals.* A few days later he asked Miss Wallace if she could visit. "I will—what? Put the MS in your hands, with the places to skip *marked*? No, I won't trust you quite that far," he wrote. "Paine enjoys it, but Paine is going to be damned one of these days, I suppose."

Because temperament and circumstance determined human conduct, Clemens reasoned, Adam and Eve and all their descendants must be blameless, not fallen. The idea of original sin made no sense. Nor was any prayer of man's ever an-swered. Heaven promised nothing that man actually valued. It granted no ground to intellect, and hymn singing and endless prayers took the place of copulation, the pleasure both men and women prized most of all. The "goody-goody ab-stract morals" of the Bible, he wrote, were mere words. Fleeting moments of happiness could not compare with "long-drawn miseries, griefs, perils, horrors, disappointments, defects, humiliations and despairs," all of which argued against a beneficent God. There was never "an intelligent person of the age of sixty who would consent to live his life over again." In short, Clemens gave the trained Presbyterian conscience a good thumping, and faced old age and death without the slightest sign of flinching.[7]

William Dean Howells continued to encourage him, and finally visited Stormfield (FIG. 55). After downhearted days, Howells wrote later, he turned to Mark Twain's books for nighttime cheer. He knew how ill Clemens had become. "There never was anybody like you," Howells wrote, "and there won't be."[8]

Bermuda at last appeared dimly on the horizon. "I haven't been well for the past 5 months, & so I haven't stirred from home," Clemens wrote Dorothy Quick on November 18, "but now I've got to make a trip, by the doctor's orders. I don't want to. But I must obey, I suppose. I sail for Bermuda day after tomorrow, with my secretary Mr. Paine for company. Perhaps we shall be back by the middle of December." When the *Bermudian* encountered rough seas it was

FIGURE 55. William Dean Howells with Clemens at Stormfield, March 1909 (courtesy the Mark Twain Project, the Bancroft Library).

Paine who took ill, not Clemens. They reached the Islands on Monday, November 22, ahead of the season, and registered at the Hamilton Hotel. Confined by the rainy day, Clemens discussed the possibility of a new planet. To his mind, even if life was governed by the same great laws of nature that so perfectly regulated celestial movement, the vast dimensions of outer space signified the minuscule importance of the human race. More than thirty years earlier, he had written of Tom Sawyer being as thrilled "as an astronomer feels who has discovered a new planet." Mathematical studies of perturbations in the orbit of Uranus now led Sir Percival Lowell to postulate an unseen planet beyond Neptune. "I believe in the new planet," Mark Twain impishly wrote earlier in 1909. "I am so sensitively constructed that I perturbate when any other planet is disturbed. This has been going on all my life. It only happens in the watermelon season. . . . I know there *is* a new planet. I know it because I don't perturbate for nothing."[9]

Clemens and Paine arrived on the Islands without being expected, Marion Allen noted in her memoir. When the weather finally cleared they took long carriage rides, "wandering at will," Paine wrote, "among the labyrinth of blossom-bordered, perfectly kept roadways of a dainty paradise" (FIG. 56).[10] After three days at the hotel, Clemens joined the Allen family for Thanksgiving dinner. He felt so welcome at Bay House that he stayed there until he left the Islands (FIG. 57). Clemens enjoyed greater privacy and the peace of long vistas over the Great Sound (FIG. 58). Any view, he thought, should have water. Mrs. Allen wrote that he so loved the sea, he "would have come for the voyage alone." As a Thanksgiving present, Clemens gave Helen an inscribed copy of *Extract from Captain Stormfield's Visit to Heaven,* which had just been published as a book. The next day he wrote his daughter Clara:

> I do hope Jean & the house are getting along well, for I don't feel a bit like leaving this peaceful refuge. . . . Everything—weather included—is in perfection here now. Paine & I drive in a light victoria about 3 hours every day, over the smooth hard roads, with the dainty blues & greens & purples of the sea always in sight. We have charming rooms in the new part of the hotel, & the table is very very good. I shall stay a good deal, both nights & days, with the Allens, but shall keep my hotel-quarters all the time. I am declining all social invitations to be out at night or late in the afternoon, but I'm going to Government House this afternoon, for that invitation has the quality of a command.

FIGURE 56. Bermuda byways, about 1910.

Mrs. Allen graciously accommodated her household to Clemens's routine. He seldom dressed before lunchtime, she wrote:

> He usually spent his mornings with his books. His books and his cigars were always with him. His bed was covered with books, manuscripts, and writing materials, while at the head of his bed stood a table with all kinds of smoking paraphernalia except cigarettes. Any spare moments were spent in reading, night or day; and he often had a book with him on the chance of an unoccupied moment. Carlyle's French Revolution, Pepys's Diary, Kipling's works, reference books of science, were always at hand, besides the late books of note sent him by every mail from Harper's Brothers.

He became interested in the history of the Islands, and kept at his bedside J. H. Lefroy's massive *Memorials of the Discovery and Early Settlement of the Bermudas or Somers Islands, 1515–1685,* in two volumes.[11] He was working on an article, "The Turning Point of My Life," which Howells solicited for *Harper's Bazar.* Earlier, at Stormfield, he had read passages to his daughter Jean and Paine. Chagrined at

FIGURE 57. Bay House, Pembroke Parish.

FIGURE 58. Vista from Bay House.

their disappointment, he suffered another angina attack, and Paine gave him what then passed for a treatment, drafts of steaming-hot drinking water. In Bermuda he continued to revise the essay. He added two startling paragraphs:

> Necessarily the scene of the real turning point of my life (and of yours) was the Garden of Eden. It was there that the first link was forged of the chain that was ultimately to lead to the emptying of me into the literary guild. Adam's *temperament* was the first command the Deity ever issued to a human being on this planet. And it was the only command Adam would *never* be able to disobey. It said, "Be weak, be water, be characterless, be cheaply persuadable." The later command, to let the fruit alone, was certain to be disobeyed. Not by Adam himself, but by his *temperament*—which he did not create and had no authority over. For the *temperament* is the man; the thing tricked out with clothes and named Man, is merely its Shadow, nothing more. The law of the tiger's temperament is, Thou shalt kill; the law of the sheep's temperament is, Thou shalt not kill. To issue later commands requiring the tiger to let the fat stranger alone, and requiring the sheep to imbue its hands in the blood of the lion is not worth while, for those commands *can't* be obeyed. They would invite to violations of the law of *temperament,* which is supreme, and takes precedence of all other authorities. I cannot help feeling disappointed in Adam and Eve. That is, in their temperaments. Not in *them,* poor helpless young creatures—afflicted with temperaments made out of butter; which butter was commanded to get into contact with fire and *be melted.* What I cannot help wishing is, that Adam and Eve had been postponed, and Martin Luther and Joan of Arc put in their place—that splendid pair equipped with temperaments not made of butter, but of asbestos. By neither sugary persuasions nor by hellfire could Satan have beguiled *them* to eat the apple.

> There would have been results! Indeed yes. The apple would be intact today: there would be no human race; there would be no *you;* there would be no *me.* And the old, old creation-dawn scheme of ultimately launching me into the literary guild would have been defeated.[12]

Every afternoon a driver named Clifford Trott appeared at the Hamilton Hotel to convey Paine down the hill and over to Bay House. Clemens now preferred to ride to the South Shore, and particularly Devonshire Bay. His seventy-fourth birthday came on Tuesday, November 30. Paine arrived a little early, bearing a gift of cuff links. He found Clemens in a good mood:

> It was rather gloomy outside, so we remained indoors by the fire and played cards, game after game of hearts, at which he excelled, and he was usually kept happy by winning. There were no visitors, and after dinner Helen asked him to read some of her favorite episodes from *Tom Sawyer,* so he read the whitewashing scene, Peter and the Pain-killer, and such chapters until tea-time. Then there was a birthday cake, and afterward cigars and talk and a quiet fireside evening.
>
> Once, in the course of his talk, he forgot a word and denounced his poor memory:
>
> "I'll forget the Lord's middle name some time," he declared, "right in the midst of a storm, when I need all the help I can get."[13]

On fair afternoons Clemens liked to take tea at one of the beaches, Mrs. Allen recalled, and join "in the children's games of tag, hop-scotch, or hide-and-seek." Nearly every Sunday he went to Prospect for the military band concerts. Once he had become a friend of the bandmaster, the entire program might consist of pieces Clemens suggested. He was very happy to be able to stay until the eighteenth, he wrote Jean on December 6; the change of scene produced a wholesome effect on his "mental-will." The news of the great world no longer engaged him, Clemens wrote. "The *Times* & the *Herald* have been at my elbow 2 days, now—unopened," he said. "The sight of a newspaper stirs not a single quiver of interest in me."

He wrote Clara the same day:

> I do not seem to be in the world or of it at all. Its affairs are not mine. Never in my life before, perhaps, have I had such a strong sense of being *severed* from the world, & the bridges all swept away. Even the billiard table has no interest for me. Paine & I have played only once. I lie in bed until past noon (breakfast in bed). I am the guest of the Allens. They wouldn't let me remain at the hotel—for that I am very thankful. For you *can't* make a home out of a hotel, & I can't be completely satisfied outside of a home. This one numbers 6 members, & is just the right size:

Mr. and Mrs. Allen, Helen; a cat, a dog, & me. We drive 3 hours, afternoons; after dinner I help Helen get her lessons; she goes to bed at 8 & the rest of us at 9.

A few days before his departure, Clemens wrote Francesca that his contentment in Bermuda had driven away the "dyspeptic pain" in his chest. He and Paine sailed from Hamilton on the *Bermudian* on Saturday, December 18. The next day, at sea, Clemens wrote Mrs. Allen:

This is not a comfortable voyage. We plunged into heavy seas before the waving handkerchiefs & the flag were an hour out of sight & nine-tenths of the passengers were abed before dinner time. Paine succumbed early, & got extravagantly seasick, & that other pain (the one in my breast) kept me entertained until 3 this morning. There is still enough sea to make writing difficult. . . . I wish I was back in that hospitable Bay House. What a contrast its comfort is to the dismal ship!

FIGURE 59. Clemens arrives at New York, December 20, 1909 (courtesy the Mark Twain Project, the Bancroft Library).

In a separate note to Helen he said the day was rainy, blustery, cold, clammy, and rough. Clemens warned her—she was now fifteen—about her boyfriend, Arthur, whom he characterized as that "snake in the grass, that precocious criminal, that ultimate decoration of the gallows! What a murderous face he has. For one so young."

He was still out of sorts when the ship reached New York on Monday, December 20 (FIG. 59). "I am through with work for this life and this world," he told the press. His health did not permit any more speech making, he said, and he did not intend to write more books.[14] Such frank talk fueled rumors that Mark Twain was dangerously ill. Jean worried that Clara, who had gone to Germany to pursue her career as a contralto, might be alarmed by news reports. She urged her father to issue a formal statement to the press.

He was not looking for pity, and on December 23 he obliged her: "I hear the newspapers say I am dying. The charge is not true. I would not do such a thing at my time of life. I am behaving as good as I can. Merry Christmas to everybody!"

VIII

Islands of the Blest, 1910

Later that day, Clemens told Jean he was thinking about a trip to Bermuda in February to get "blessedly out of the clash & turmoil again for another month." Jean approved, but said that if he could wait until March, she and Katy Leary, their longtime family servant, would go along. The plan was to rent a furnished house on the Islands, with servants. Although for years she had been moody and withdrawn, often difficult and subject to epileptic seizures, Jean now managed the household competently, and helped her father as a secretary. Friday morning, the day before Christmas, she suffered another seizure, then a heart attack, and died in her bath.

Much like Alexander Pope, who said he wrote *To help me thro' this long Disease, my Life,* Clemens responded to a death in his family by writing about it. His immediate account of the death of Jean, he told Paine, could stand as the final chapter of his autobiography:[1]

I lost Susy thirteen years ago; I lost her mother—her incomparable mother!—five & a half years ago; Clara has gone away to live in Europe; & now I have lost Jean. How poor I am, who was once so rich! . . . Jean lies yonder, I sit here; we are strangers under our own roof; we kissed hands good-by at this door last night—& it was forever, we never suspecting it. She lies there, & I sit here—writing, busying myself to keep my heart from breaking. . . .

Would I bring her back to life if I could do it? I would not . . . for she has been enriched with the most precious of all gifts—that gift which makes all other gifts mean & poor—death. I have never wanted any released friend of mine restored to life since I reached manhood. . . .

Why did I build this house, two years ago? To shelter this vast emptiness? How foolish I was. But I shall stay in it. . . . Jean's spirit will make it beautiful for me always.

A few days later, he wrote to a friend that his grief would give way to gratitude for Jean's release "from the ungentle captivity of this life." The newspapers were mistaken about his own health, Clemens said, because he had "brought it back from Bermuda *perfect.*"

Nearly everyone was now gone. Miss Lyon and Ashcroft had married in March, and had been dismissed soon afterward. Jean's death left only Paine and his wife to manage the household. They moved with their youngest daughter from their own home, and occupied Jean's rooms at Stormfield. Now that Jean was safe, Clemens wrote Clara on December 29, he would never again be melancholy: "You see, I was in such distress when I came to realize that you were gone far away & no one stood between her & danger but me—& I could die at any moment, & *then*—oh then what would become of her! For she was wilful, you know, & would not have been governable." Paine assumed his duties with his usual skill. He wrote William H. Allen that Clemens might soon be arriving in Bermuda. "Of course, one can never tell just what Mr. Clemens is going to do, as he is impulsive," Paine said, "but I feel pretty sure he will want to make another Bermuda trip before the winter is over."[2]

New Year's caught Clemens ill with a cold. It was his first in two years, he wrote Miss Wallace. "The pain in my breast has come back," he said, "so I am leaving for Bermuda next Wednesday [January 5], for an indefinite stay." Paine wrote Allen again on January 3:

For Mr. Clemens, I want to say that he is more than anxious to go to your house during his stay in Bermuda, for he does not like hotel life . . . but he feels he could not take advantage of this generosity on your part for any length of time without some compensation. . . .

Now, as to other matters; you have already realized, of course, that Mr. Clemens has to be protected from the great number of people who wish to use him as the means of their own social advancement, or as an ornament for their drawing-rooms and dinner tables. . . .

He is also to be guarded from business propositions of every sort—schemes, plans, investments, and the like. These things have been his undoing through a long period of years. . . . He does not wish ever to make an investment again. But, as I have said, he is impulsive, enthusiastic, and likely to fall in with the suggestion of a plan which would only mean discomfort, worry and nightmare for him later on, and he has had enough of such things. . . .[3]

You have, of course, already realized that Mr. Clemens's nature, like his genius, is an unusual one. His likes and dislikes are erratic, quickly formed, and like railroad time-tables, "subject to change without notice." The man or woman he is apparently delighted with today, he may not care to see tomorrow at all, and vice versa. . . .

I need not make any suggestion as to the care of his health, only that I am sending Claude [Benchotte], his valet (who will be provided for at the hotel), a bottle of medicine to be given him only if the pain in his breast should be very severe indeed, and not relievable by hot water treatment. . . .

It is possible of course, that you may have company, and will not be able to take care of him at all for the present, in which case he will try to stand the hotel as best he can; but he is very fond of your roof-tree, and all that it shelters, and Bermuda just now beckons to him as does no other locality in the world.

Clemens took the train to New York on Tuesday, January 4, and had dinner that night with Howells and Paine at the home of Edward E. Loomis, who was married to Livy's niece, Julia O. Langdon. Howells first met Clemens more than forty years earlier, shortly after he reviewed *The Innocents Abroad* and noted its impudence, sauciness, and irreverence. He also wrote then in the *Atlantic Monthly* that he found "an amount of pure human nature in the book that rarely gets into literature." The two old friends were now about to part forever. Howells would soon recall that "the last time I saw him alive was made memorable to me by the kind, clear judicial sense with which he explained and justified the labor-unions as the sole present help of the weak against the strong."[4]

The *Bermudian* sailed on Wednesday. After the ship anchored at Hamilton on Friday, January 7, Clemens began the first of ninety-five days on the Islands, his longest stay. He wore a black mourning band on his left arm, and when he wrote Loomis that day from Bay House he used stationery bordered in black. "I have just arrived," he said, "& am very much pleased with the weather." The same day, he wrote to Frederick Duneka of Harper & Brothers to ask for three books. Clemens resumed his pattern of reading and writing in the mornings, then taking carriage rides in the afternoons. Helen Allen's blurry snapshots sometimes showed him dressed in white—"my dontcareadamnsuit," he called it—and seated in a rocker on the Bay House lawn, smoking. When he showed Mrs. Allen his chapter on the death of Jean, saying it was the last he would ever write, tears welled in his eyes. Occasionally he suffered chest pains, she wrote, but a cup of almost boiling water usually relieved him at once, "and two or three more were sure to do so." In spite of his angina, and the serenity of Bay House (so close to town, but unknown to most Bermudians even today), Clemens continued to make excursions. Mrs. Allen watched over him and took along a thermos of hot water.

Helen and her mother went with Clemens to a military lecture at Prospect on January 10. The speaker had sent a special invitation, saying he wished to address in particular Mark Twain, "the greatest living master of the platform-art." They were greeted by Lt.-Gen. Frederick Walter Kitchener, the governor of Bermuda and a brother of Horatio Herbert Kitchener of Khartoum, commander in chief during much of the South African War of 1899 to 1902. Clemens worried that on a previous occasion he had committed a breach of etiquette. He wrote Paine the next day to express relief that the governor was "apparently as glad to see me as he said he was." That night, Clemens planned to dine with the commandant of the *Carnegie,* who promised to arrange a private tour of his ship.[5]

Some days later, he wrote Paine that he had just heard from Clara: "She is pretty desolate now after Jean's emancipation—the only kindness that God ever did that poor, unoffending child in all her hard life." Clemens enclosed what he called a gorgeous letter from Howells, about "The Turning Point of My Life":

While your wonderful words are warm in my mind yet I want to tell you what you know already: that you never wrote anything greater, finer, than that turning-point paper of yours.

I shall feel it honor enough if they put on my tombstone "He was born in the same Century and general Section of middle western country with

Dr. S. L. Clemens, Oxon., and had his Degree three years before him through a Mistake of the University."

I hope you are worse. You will never be riper for a purely intellectual life, and it is a pity to have you lagging along with a wornout material body on top of your soul.

Across the top of the letter, Clemens wrote: "I reckon this spontaneous outburst by the first critic of the day is good to keep, ain't it, Paine?"[6]

The death of Jean, like that of his infant son, Langdon, and his younger brother Henry, continued to stir Clemens's conscience. He had favored Susy over his other daughters, and had spent little time with Jean. And now, as he wrote a friend on January 26, his entire family had disappeared:

I fled to Bermuda when the disaster fell—the *double* disaster, for Clara was gone into permanent exile 13 days before Jean was set free from the swindle of this life. Stormfield was a desolation. Its charm all gone & I could not stay there.

My ship has gone down, but my raft has landed me in the Islands of the Blest, & I am as happy as any other shipwrecked sailor ever was. I shan't go "home" till . . . I don't know when—There's no hurry. Hurry? Why, there's no hurry about *anything*, suddenly the hurry has all gone out of my life.[7]

Nothing of his sorrow was associated with Bermuda, he said. Yet the contentment at Bay House sometimes was interrupted. Clemens once inadvertently hurt Helen's feelings. "That is always my way," he told her mother. "I hurt those whom I love: now I suppose I must lose all three of you just when I need you the most."

Miss Wallace continued to correspond, hoping in her gentle way that Clemens would grow to see the world in a golden light. She got nowhere. He wrote her on January 26:

No, revelation—of a valuable sort—does not come through sorrow when one is old. Before 70 the whole satire & swindle of life has been revealed—to all except the wilfully or constitutionally dull. What a silly invention human life is! . . . Do I "know more" than I knew before? Oh,

hell no! There was nothing to learn, (about hereafters & other-such un-
desirables), there has never *been* anything to learn & know about those
insulting mysteries.[8]

Clemens persisted in that vein as he explored the work of Will N. Harben, a
southern novelist who had attended his seventieth birthday banquet at Delmonico's. Harben's characters, Howells had written, spoke as though they had
never been in books before. "I believe you will end by liking poor old Harben as
much as I do," he wrote Clemens on February 11. "He didn't make North
Georgia; he only made a likeness of it. Don't shoot the artist." Clemens scribbled in his notebook that Harben had faults, but recognized "that the *man* does
not act, but only his disposition & circumstances, *he* being merely the weather-
cock that these influences blow upon":

> Also I think he dimly perceives that no feature of God's character exceeds
> in magnitude & virility the same feature of man's character except MA-
> LIGNITY. The pulpit claims that Man has in him the "divine" spark. If he
> has, this is it.
>
> H[arben] also dimly perceives another great fact which is invisible to the
> blind pulpit—to-wit, that no God & no man is ever moved to action by
> any impulse but to content his own spirit. *Selfishness* . . . The pulpit deals
> in falsehood & foolishness when it chatters about *un*selfishness. Neither
> in heaven nor on the earth is there any such thing as *un*selfishness. Men
> come *nearer* to doing unselfish things than the gods have ever done.
>
> The gods never *give* anything—they always *sell.* At war prices.
>
> *"Believe on me"*—& ye shall be saved. Those are the terms.
>
> *"Come unto me,"* ye that are weary & I will gave you rest. That is, worship
> me.
>
> *"Except ye believe on me"*—you are damned. Pay up! if you want to be
> saved.

Howells wrote later that Clemens's "unreligion" reached back many years: "The
faith he had been taught in his childhood passed with his childhood."[9]

In spite of such ruminations, Clemens continued to savor the outdoors, always the greatest of Bermuda's attractions. He also enjoyed society; at the end of January he asked Paine to send him two hundred visiting cards. Sometimes in the afternoon he went to the Little Green Door Tea Garden, a rustic place by Pitt's Bay Road that overlooked the harbor. He cut a striking figure at a Government House party to honor German naval officers, the *Royal Gazette* reported on January 31, and appeared with Governor Kitchener again on February 3 for a party at Norwood, the seaside home of Mr. and Mrs. Hastings Outerbridge, near Bailey's Bay. Mildred Howells, who arrived in Hamilton at the end of January, joined Clemens, Mr. and Mrs. Allen, and other guests for a motorboat excursion on February 4. "Several hours' swift skimming over ravishing blue seas, a brilliant sun; also a couple of hours of picnicking & lazying under the cedars in a secluded place," Clemens wrote Paine.

He dreaded being alone, Mrs. Allen noted, and was happy to be with friends. He still ventured out at night, and to the hotels Paine thought he meant to avoid. Usually he went to the Hamilton, where Claude was staying. "On almost any dance or concert night," the *Royal Gazette* reported on February 12, "he may be seen seated in one of the parlours surrounded by admiring friends. He has an especial fondness for children and they in their turn love him and hover around him." That night the mayor of St. George hosted a dinner at the hotel for the officers of a French squadron, and Mark Twain was celebrated as a special guest. Woodrow Wilson arrived for his winter holiday on Monday, February 14. He registered at the Hamilton Hotel, and crossed the harbor to Paget for a melancholy walk toward Shoreby, all the while thinking about the absent Mrs. Peck. He wrote his wife that he found relief from his troubles at Princeton—"the struggle all night with college foes, the sessions of hostile trustees, the confused war of argument and insinuation"—because Bermuda afforded peace and exquisite weather with healing sea breezes. Tuesday night at the hotel he met Clemens, who was equally content to be staying in Bermuda: "What he particularly rejoices in having got rid of is (for some reason) trolley cars and (quite reasonably) newspapers and newspaper reporters. He seems weaker than when I last saw him, but very well. He speaks of the tragical death of his daughter with touching simplicity. He is certainly one of the most human of men. . . . He evidently wants me to call on him and I shall of course do so. 'Calling' is easy and natural here!"[10]

Clemens by now regarded Paine as his business agent, and was satisfied with his performance. Paine soon noticed that the King was beginning to use Helen Allen as his secretary, and was dictating his letters. Sunday night, February 20, Clemens dined with friends at the Princess Hotel, and the next night he went to the Hamilton Hotel for a party hosted by Mrs. Moncure Robinson of Philadelphia. But he was not well, and had just written to Mary Benjamin Rogers, the wife of H. H. Rogers Jr.:

Would you expect a person to catch a bronchial cold in Bermuda? Well, I have achieved that miracle. A lady brought it from America & I sat at a bridge table with her four days ago & caught it, & carried it to bed & was not on my feet again until I turned out to keep that dinner-engagement yesterday evening. That was my very first game of bridge. It is a bad-luck game. It is not even lucky when you try, out of kindness, to help other people pass the time pleasantly when they are playing it. I have suffered violence for that act of benevolence. . . .

My health is blemishless except for the pain in my breast. That is permanent, I suppose. It doesn't allow me to work, & it doesn't allow me to walk even so much as a hundred yards; but as it lets me do all the things I want to do, it is not an encumbrance.

As his bronchitis lingered, Clemens rested in the morning sunshine. He took shorter carriage rides in the afternoon, and at night used a vaporizer recommended by Wilson, who had been invited to Bay House for a piano recital. The prospect of a formal musical event so unnerved Clemens that he fired a letter to Paine:

It is 2:30 in the morning & I am writing because I can't sleep. I can't sleep because a professional pianist is coming to-morrow afternoon *to play for me.* My God! . . . I would rather have a leg amputated. I knew he was coming, but I never dreamed it was to play for *me.* When I heard the horrible news 4 hours ago, be d—d if I didn't come near screaming. I meant to slip out and be absent, but now I can't. Don't pray for me. The thing is just as d—d bad as it can be already.

He was also disturbed by learning that Clara and her husband hoped to secure an invitation to Easter services at St. Peter's in Rome. He asked George Harvey to intercede for Clara, but denounced "that odious Church, whose history would disgrace hell, & whose birth was the profoundest calamity which has ever befallen the human race except for the birth of Christ." Once again, he pleaded with Colonel Harvey to *"run down here."* Yet his bronchitis made it troublesome even to converse, and on February 25 he ended a three-page note to Paine by dictating: "I am tired and must stop."

The siege of bronchitis lasted for weeks. Tired though he was, Clemens courteously received a journalist by the unlikely name of Mildred Champagne. She appeared at Bay House on a pony, and tipped a barefoot Bermudian lad after he confirmed that Mark Twain was staying there. After she rapped at the front door and got no answer, she walked around the house and through a glass door spied Clemens. He was wearing a white linen suit, the mourning band still on his arm, and lying on a bed with books spread before him. "His face looked small and pinched and ill," she wrote:

And then he started to cough, a miserable nerve-wracking cough that shook the whole of his slight frame, and left him nervous and trembling, and a trifle irritated. He held his hand on his chest.

"I don't see anybody," he said. "Nobody, nobody. I'm not—er—extravagantly well. I—er—I bark, bark, bark all the time. I can't talk to anybody. Now, mind you, I didn't get this cough in Bermuda. Somebody kindly imported it for me from the United States."

I expressed my sympathy. He was sweet again, and mollified.

"Have you seen the Crystal Cave yet?" he asked. "Or the Aquarium?"

I said, "No. I came to see you first." . . .

"Well, you shouldn't have seen me first," he said quickly. "I run an opposition show to the Crystal Cave and the Aquarium. But they're not shucks to me. I'm lots better. I give them their money's worth. But you should see them. Then you will appreciate me."

But then he asked not to be recommended to sightseers:

"I'm too old a bird to be caught. Besides, I'm going to charge an admission fee. It's a shilling a look." He coughed again that terrible, racking cough that left him weak and gasping after each onslaught. "The price is going up—up—all—the time—," he continued weakly. "To-morrow it will be two shillings—the next day—three." . . .

I saw Mark Twain again before I left Bermuda. His face was paler than when I had first seen him, and he was more composed. I inquired solicitously after his health, and he thanked me.

"I am much better," he replied. "I suppose I am as well as could be expected of a man of my age and circumstances. Fairly well—but not extravagantly well—you understand."[11]

When he seemed to recover, Clemens left Bay House to watch the matches during cricket week, even on cold and windy days. He ran off "just as a bad boy would when he saw his chance," Mrs. Allen wrote. One day he went to a horse race. Wilson called again on March 3, two days before sailing from the Islands, and spent the afternoon with Clemens. They played miniature golf on the Bay House lawn, which had a green with nine holes. Clemens greatly impressed Mrs. Allen by referring to Wilson as the next president of the United States; but George Harvey had proposed Wilson for the presidency as early as 1906, and it was in Harvey's home that Wilson would soon be offered the Democratic nomination for governor of New Jersey.

Clemens was becoming noticeably more ill. The "blind voyage," as he called life, was almost over.[12] One day he set out with Mrs. Allen to attend another event for the Cottage Hospital. Just as they reached Government House, where the benefit was being held, Clemens suffered chest pains so severe he could not talk. He took the hot water remedy and finally reached the tea table. Dorothy Quick had arrived in Bermuda with her mother. When they registered at the Hamilton Hotel, she recalled many years later, they saw Clemens crossing the lobby. "He looked his age for the first time," she wrote. "In fact, he seemed suddenly to have grown years older and very worn. The once erect figure was a little stooped." They planned to visit him at Bay House on March 12, but left the Islands abruptly that day, after Mrs. Quick learned of the death of her brother. Dorothy told Clemens that without his guidance she had made no further literary efforts:

He shook his head sadly and wisely. "No matter what happens, Dorothy dear, you must write: cataclysms, sorrow, pain, nothing must interfere with the expression of a talent that should have its outlet. A trade that is once taken up must be followed to the bitter end. It's your job in life and you must see that it is well done."

His eyes were half-closed as he spoke, and it seemed as though he were talking more to himself than to me.[13]

Clemens still had good hours. On the day Dorothy and her mother left he took an old, familiar drive. "You ought to be here *now*!" he wrote Miss Wallace. "The weather is divine; & you know what it is to drive along the North Shore in such weather & watch the sun paint the waters. We had that happiness today. The joy of it never stales." He had enough energy that day to compose at least four other letters. To a correspondent who had sent him her picture, he wrote:

> No doubt I shall go home one of these days—possibly a month hence, or two months. Time drifts along, here, at about the gait I like. There are no excitements, & I don't want any. Twice a week we go to hear the garrison band play; twice a week I go to hear the hotel string-bands play, & look on while the multitude dances; a drive once a day, & now & then a sail—these are my activities & they are sufficient. I do not go out to dinner oftener than once a week, & then only to feed with friends. When there's a stranger I don't go. There are no newspapers, no telegrams, no mobiles, no trolleys, no trams, no railways, no theatres, no lectures, no riots, no murders, no fires, no burglaries, no offences of any kind, no follies but church, & I don't go there. I think I could live here always & be contented. The weekly steamer passes by my window Friday mornings, & again next day outward bound—& that's the only disturbance.
>
> You go to heaven if you want to—I'd druther stay here.[14]

A renewed sense of lifelong achievement reinforced Clemens's feeling of well-being. He told Clara that he had turned to *A Connecticut Yankee in King Arthur's Court* for the first time in more than twenty years. "I am prodigiously pleased with it—a most gratifying surprise," Clemens wrote. He likewise took pride again in the literary judgments of William Lyon Phelps, a professor at Yale. Phelps sent Clemens a copy of his new collection, titled *Essays on Modern Novelists*. His essay on Mark Twain had first appeared in July 1907, just after Clemens received his degree from Oxford. Although once regarded merely as a humorist, Phelps wrote, Mark Twain now stood as "our foremost living American writer":

> I wish that Mr. Howells might live forever, and give to every generation the pure intellectual joy that he has given to ours. But the natural endowment of Mark Twain is still greater. Mr. Howells has made the most of himself; God has done it all for Mark Twain. If there be a living

American writer touched with true genius, whose books glow with the divine fire, it is he. He has always been a conscientious artist; but no amount of industry could ever have produced a "Huckleberry Finn." . . . Mark Twain is through and through American. If foreigners really wish to know the American spirit, let them read Mark Twain. He is far more American than their favorite specimen, Walt Whitman.[15]

Clemens wrote Phelps on March 12 that he had read his book in a single night, and without regret for a lost night of sleep. "I am glad if I deserve what you have said about me; & even if I don't I am proud & well contented, since you *think* I deserve it." But in writing Miss Wallace, who attempted to reassure him with intimations of the afterlife, he lost all patience: "You 'know there are worlds still unexplored,' do you? Very well, then—you *don't*. Why do you want to talk like that, & wither a person's hopes? Isn't this life enough for you? Do you wish to continue the foolishness somewhere else? Damnation, you depress me!"[16]

More than forty years had passed since Clemens first saw Bermuda, the answer to a civilization that "destroyed the simplicity and repose of life . . . with the money-fever, sordid ideals, vulgar ambitions, and the sleep which does not refresh."[17] He was happy when Robert J. Collier and his young wife arrived on March 11, and he wrote Clara that he would not go home to Stormfield until the end of April, when he could see "the new leafage unfold upon the trees." In another letter to Paine, dictated on March 17–18, he cheerfully talked about taking Allen's post as vice-consul, and thanked Colonel Harvey for getting Clara into "the Easter dissipations at Rome." He made light of his illness. "I have been coughing for some weeks," Clemens said, "but there is not enough of this cough to inconvenience me. The pain in my breast still abides with me, but it troubles me very little."

At the same time, Paine sensed trouble. He sent an urgent note to Helen's father: "Won't you please write me privately just what Mr. Clemens's health condition is?" Collier was back in New York on March 21. "I saw Mr. Clemens nearly every day that I spent on the island, and talked with him," he said. "In my opinion he is better than I have seen him at any time during the last four years."[18] Of course he was not telling the truth; the next day, as Clemens was having lunch on Agar's Island, he suffered what Mrs. Allen termed a dangerous attack. "From this time on, he slept but little," she wrote, "and the shortness of breath began." Clemens valiantly refused to have a nurse. He wrote Clara on March 24 that he had spent three days in his room trying to tame the pains.

They were caused by "extravagant & inexcusable imprudences in feeding," he pretended. For the first time, he took prescription medicine, morphine. "My father died this day 63 years ago," Clemens mused. "I remember all about it quite clearly."

The next day he dictated a letter to Paine:

> We are booked to sail in the *Bermudian* April 23rd, but don't tell anybody. I don't want it known. I may have to go sooner if the pain in my breast doesn't mend its ways pretty considerably.
>
> I don't want to die here, for this is an unkind place for a person in that condition. I should have to lay in the undertaker's cellar until the ship would remove me, & it is dark down there & unpleasant. The Colliers will meet me on the pier & I may stay with them a week or two before going home. It all depends on the breast pain. I don't want to die there. I am growing more & more particular about the place.

A few days later, he wrote Paine about having a most uncomfortable time with the breast pain, "which turns out to be an affection of the heart, just as I originally suspected." Paine learned from Allen that Clemens's condition was considered critical. He sailed from New York on Saturday, April 2. The next day, Clemens received a puzzling cablegram:

> THE CLOWNS OF BARNUM AND BAILEYS CIRCUS RECOGNIZING YOU AS THE WORLDS GREATEST LAUGHMAKER WILL CONSIDER IT AN HONOR IF YOU WILL BE THEIR LUNCHEON GUEST AT MADISON SQUARE GARDEN SUNDAY AFTERNOON APRIL THIRD AT TWO.

He immediately responded: "I am very sorry, but all last week's dates are full. I will gladly come week before last, if that will answer." Neither age nor illness could dull his wit.[19]

Paine reached Bay House on Monday morning, April 4, and came upon Clemens seated in his dressing gown. For a few days, the King appeared relatively well. They discussed a piece of land Clemens had given to Jean but not legally conveyed. As directed, Paine had sold it, for six thousand dollars. Clemens dictated a letter to his attorney, Charles T. Lark, instructing that the money be used for the Mark Twain Library in Redding. The building was to be named the Jean L. Clemens Memorial. Clemens talked to Paine about books he was reading, and rested in bed or on the lawn. "I found that he had been really very much alive during those three months," Paine said, "too much for his own good, sometimes—for he had not been careful of his hours or his diet, and had suffered in consequence." On one of his outings, the King had been pressed into accepting a speaking engagement at a woman's club. He soothed his irritation by writing "Etiquette for the Afterlife," intended mainly for Paine's amusement:

Upon arrival in heaven do not speak to St. Peter until spoken to. It is not your place to begin. . . .

When applying for a ticket, avoid trying to make conversation. St. Peter is hard-worked and has no time for conversation. If you *must* talk, let the weather alone. St. Peter cares not a damn for the weather. And don't ask him what time the 4:30 train goes; there aren't any trains in heaven, except through trains for the other place, and the less information you get about them, the better for you.

You can ask him for his autograph—there is no harm in that—but be careful and don't remark that it is one of the penalties of greatness. He has heard *that* before. . . .

Leave your dog outside. Heaven goes by favor. If it went by merit, you would stay out & the dog would go in.

Keep off the grass.[20]

The captain of the *Bermudian* knew where Clemens was staying and that he was ill. As the King waited by the window, the ship sailed past Cockle Point on Saturday morning, April 9, and saluted him with two short whistles. In gratitude for her hospitality, Clemens had given Marion Allen a copy of his book *Is Shakespeare Dead?* published the previous April. Now he inscribed for her a photograph of himself. "To Mrs. William H. Allen," he wrote, "with the high esteem & guarded affection of Mark Twain, Bermuda, April 9/10." (The peculiar wording lent a slight credence to a later rumor that something untoward had occurred when he was ill at Bay House.)[21] When he came to leave the Islands, on Tuesday, April 12, he was too weak to be dressed. Wrapped in his coat and a few rugs, Clemens was carried in a canvas chair to the SS *Corona*, then taken by the

FIGURE 60. Sunset over the Great Sound.

tender to the RMS *Oceana.* The man who had led such a violently gay and energetic life sailed from the Islands of the Blest for the last time (FIG. 60).

He reached Stormfield on April 14. Clara, who was expecting a child, arrived
a few days later. She wrote Mrs. Allen that her father was so ill he could not talk.
On Thursday, April 21, he tried to write her a note: "Dear—You did not tell me,
but I have found out that you—." He died that evening.

Appendix

Table of Days on the Islands

Eight voyages took Mark Twain to Bermuda between 1867 and 1910. Altogether, he spent 187 days on the Islands:

1867 Monday, November 11, to Friday, November 15. Sailing on the *Quaker City*, with some sixty-three excursionists returning from the Holy Land. (Four days on the Islands.)

1877 Sunday, May 20, to Thursday, May 24. On the SS *Bermuda*, with the Reverend Joseph H. Twichell. They were the only guests at Mrs. Kirkham's Private Boarding House, in Hamilton. (Four days.)

1907 Friday, January 4, to Monday, January 7. On the RMS *Bermudian*, with Reverend Twichell and Isabel V. Lyon. Stayed at the Princess Hotel, Hamilton. (Three days.)

Monday, March 18, to Tuesday, March 19. On the RMS *Bermudian*, with Miss Lyon and Miss Paddy Madden. They sleep on board. (One day.)

1908 Monday, January 27, to Monday, February 3. On the RMS *Bermudian*, with Ralph Ashcroft. Stayed at the Princess Hotel. (Seven days.)

Monday, February 24, to Saturday, April 11. On the RMS *Bermudian*, with H. H. Rogers, William E. Benjamin, Miss Lyon, and Rogers's valet. At the Princess Hotel. (Forty-seven days.)

1909   Monday, November 22, to Saturday, December 18. On the RMS *Bermudian,* with Albert Bigelow Paine. At the Hamilton Hotel briefly, then at Bay House, 4 Old Slip Lane. (Twenty-six days.)

1910   Friday, January 7, to Tuesday, April 12. On the RMS *Bermudian,* with Claude Benchotte, his valet. At Bay House. (Ninety-five days.)

Notes

Citations to Mark Twain's books published during his lifetime will be to the first American editions, conveniently reprinted in facsimile in the *Oxford Mark Twain* (New York, 1996), 29 vols. (*Mark Twain's Speeches,* the final volume, was published posthumously.) Most other references to his writings not in the Oxford series will be to the Library of America set titled *Mark Twain: Collected Tales, Sketches, Speeches, & Essays, 1852–1890* and *Mark Twain: Collected Tales, Sketches, Speeches & Essays, 1891–1910* (New York, 1992), cited as *Collected Tales* 1 and 2. Dates given for his shorter works refer to the original year of publication. All of Mark Twain's words are quoted by permission of the Mark Twain Project, Robert H. Hirst, general editor, the Bancroft Library, the University of California at Berkeley.

1. The "Long, Strange Cruise" of 1867

1. Letters of March 12, 1910, to Elizabeth Wallace and to a second, less identified correspondent. All quotations from Clemens's correspondence can be located in the electronic editions of his published and unpublished letters in the Mark Twain Papers, the Bancroft Library. Notable among other isolated but habitable places are Easter Island in the South Pacific and St. Helena Island in the Atlantic.

2. *Life on the Mississippi* (1883), 62, 166, 246. Clemens liked to say that he "confiscated" his famous pen name after the death of Capt. Isaiah Sellers, who used it in reporting river news in the *New Orleans Picayune* (ibid., 497–98), and a letter of June 24, 1874. Sellers, however, did not die until March 1864, and no evidence has been found of his having used "Mark Twain." Late in life, Clemens recalled that a depth of six feet made him shudder but the call of mark twain "took the shudder away"; see *Is Shakespeare Dead?* (1909), 65. For a steamboat drawing nine feet, however, the same call signaled danger.

3. "Caprices of Memory," *Bermuda Royal Gazette* (Hamilton), April 11, 1908; reprinted in *Mark Twain, Plymouth Rock and the Pilgrims,* edited by Charles Neider (New York, 1984), 325. Clemens was born on November 30, 1835, in the hamlet of Florida, Missouri, twenty-seven miles southwest of Hannibal, as the crow flies. Florida in recent years has numbered only two year-round residents.

4. *The Innocents Abroad* (1869), 587. In a sketch titled "Misplaced Confidence" (1870), he speaks of Hannibal schoolboys "welcoming the first steamboat of the season" (*Collected Tales,* 1:383).

5. *Mark Twain's Letters from Hawaii,* edited by A. Grove Day (New York, 1966), 52, 53, 109; *Roughing It* (1872), 463. Such comments on missionaries and legislators, reiterated in later years, show that Mark Twain from very early on was an acerbic critic of society and mankind.

6. Autobiographical dictation, April 1904. Typescripts of all his dictations are in the Mark Twain Papers, Bancroft Library.

7. "My Debut as a Literary Person" (1899), in *The Man That Corrupted Hadleyburg, and Other Stories and Essays* (1900), 85. Two other boats that set out from the *Hornet* disaster were lost at sea.

8. Letter of October 3, 1858, in Albert Bigelow Paine, *Mark Twain: A Biography,* 3 vols. (New York, 1912), 3:1592; Clara Clemens, *My Father Mark Twain* (New York, 1931), 264. As to the true source of humor, see *Following the Equator* (1897), 119. Robert Gottlieb, in "The Years with Thurber," notes that James Thurber (who also enjoyed holidays in Bermuda) once said, "I can't hide any more behind the mask of comedy that I've used all my life. . . . People are not funny; they are vicious and horrible—and so is life" (*New Yorker,* September 8, 2003, 90).

9. *Mark Twain's Letters,* vol. 5, edited by Lin Salamo and Harriet Elinor Smith (Berkeley, CA, 1997), 395n. Also see *Roughing It* (1872), 560, and "The Facts Concerning the Recent Carnival of Crime in Connecticut" (1876), in *The Stolen White Elephant, Etc.* (1882), 109, 118.

10. *Mark Twain's Travels with Mr. Brown,* edited by Franklin Walker and G. Ezra Dane (New York, 1940), 91. "To forty-nine men in fifty the Sabbath Day is a dreary, dreary bore," he wrote more than forty years later; see *Letters from the Earth,* in *What Is Man? and Other Philosophical Writings,* edited by Paul Baender (Berkeley, CA, 1973), 407.

11. For a facsimile of the second edition of the excursion prospectus, see *Mark Twain's Letters,* vol. 2, edited by Harriet Elinor Smith and Richard Bucci (Berkeley, CA, 1990), 382–84. A slightly altered version of the prospectus is in *The Innocents Abroad,* 20–23. Also see *Travels with Brown,* 111–16.

12. "Mark Twain as a Lecturer," *New York Tribune,* May 11, 1867; see *Mark Twain's Letters,* 2:418–19. House spent most of his time in Japan after 1870. He taught English, founded the *Tokio Times,* and directed the Imperial Court Orchestra. Clemens had considered "Ned" House a brilliant writer, but after a dispute over dramatizing *The Prince and the Pauper* named him to his permanent list of hated persons, and called him both a "blatherskite" and "scoundrel."

13. *New York Independent,* May 2, 1867; Erik Heyl, *Early American Steamers* (Buffalo, NY,

1953), 355; see also a letter of April 15, 1867, from Clemens to his family, and his article "About All Kinds of Ships," in *The £1,000,000 Bank-Note, and Other New Stories* (1893), 159.

14. *A Connecticut Yankee in King Arthur's Court* (1889), 219. In his story "The Facts Concerning the Recent Carnival of Crime in Connecticut," conscience is vividly embodied as a "shabby dwarf" and "vile bit of human rubbish," then murdered.

15. "Each man bears the entire form of man's estate," Montaigne wrote in his essay on repentance. He also wrote of "the study I am making, the subject of which is man"; see *Michel de Montaigne: The Complete Works,* translated by Donald M. Frame (New York, 2003), 584, 740. I am indebted to Professor George Hoffmann for the references. Clemens acquired a four-volume set of Montaigne's works in 1873; see Alan Gribben, *Mark Twain's Library* (Boston, 1980), 480. Nietzsche, a great admirer of Montaigne, likewise wrote that the true philosopher found in himself "a reflection and brief abstract of the whole world"; see *Untimely Meditations,* translated by R. J. Hollingdale (Cambridge, 1983), 181.

16. *New York Times,* June 9, 1867, 8.

17. *The Innocents Abroad,* 147. In *Roughing It* he speaks of "the mellow moonshine of romance" (149), and in *The American Claimant* (1892) of "romantic rubbish" (53). Descriptions by "excitable literary people," he says in *Following the Equator,* work against a "natural and rational focus" on sights and facts (570).

18. *The Innocents Abroad,* 192, 209, 220–21, 241–42.

19. Samuel E. Moffett, "Mark Twain: A Biographical Sketch," in *The $30,000 Bequest, and Other Stories* (1906), 339. His brief military experience offered an epitome of war—"the killing of strangers against whom you feel no personal animosity," Mark Twain wrote in "The Private History of a Campaign That Failed" (1885), in *Merry Tales* (1892), 44–45.

20. *New York Sun,* November 21, 1867, 2. Also see Dewey Ganzel, *Mark Twain Abroad: The Cruise of the "Quaker City"* (Chicago, 1968), chap. 9.

21. "Charles Maxwell Allen, U.S. Consul to Bermuda, 1861–1888," *Bermuda Historical Quarterly* 26 (1969): 10–11. The consulate was in St. George until being moved to Hamilton in 1872; see Walter B. Smith II, *America's Diplomats and Consuls of 1776–1865* (Washington, 1986), 132. Allen suspected that Dr. Luke Pryor Blackburn arrived in Bermuda in September 1864 to secretly ship clothing impregnated with yellow fever poison to cities in the North. Nothing came of the scandal, and Dr. Blackburn served in 1879–1883 as governor of Kentucky; see Lawrence Segel, MD, "'The Yellow Fever Plot': Germ Warfare during the Civil War," *Diagnosis* (September 2002): 47–50. In the tale titled "A Curious Experience" (1881), Mark Twain mentions rumors that rebel spies planned to send "infected clothing" into Northern towns; see *The Stolen White Elephant,* 149.

22. *The Innocents Abroad,* 647.

23. "Quaker City Journal," manuscript in the Patten Free Library, Bath, ME. A safer and more direct way to St. George's Harbor, the Town Cut, was formally opened in 1917. Captain Duncan later gave lectures on the Holy Land excursion, and in 1877 related that Clemens had been full of whisky when he applied for passage on the pilgrimage. Clemens responded by sending letters to the *New York World.* "I know him to be a canting hypocrite, filled to the chin with sham godliness, and forever oozing and dripping false piety and

pharisaical prayers," Clemens wrote. "I know his word to be worthless." See *Mark Twain to Mrs. Fairbanks,* edited by Dixon Wecter (San Marino, CA, 1949), 214.

24. Marvell's poem is variously titled "Bermudas" and "The Emigrants"; see also *Tom Moore's Bermuda Poems and Notes,* edited by William Zuill (Hamilton, Bermuda, n.d.), 9. For the bizarre story of Byron's destroyed manuscript, see Doris Langley Moore, "The Burning of Lord Byron's Memoirs," *Atlantic* (August 1959): 27–37.

25. Fifty-three sunken vessels are located by Daniel Berg and Denise Berg in *Bermuda Shipwrecks* (East Rockaway, NY, 1991). In 1936, the *Cristobal Colon,* a luxury cruise liner five hundred feet long, became the largest vessel wrecked on the Bermuda reefs.

26. Terry Tucker, *Bermuda—Unintended Destination, 1609–1610* (Bermuda, 1978), 23, 24, 30. In early years, the Bermudas were cleverly called the "Sommer Islands" to signify both Sir George Somers and the warm climate.

27. Anthony Trollope, *The West Indies and the Spanish Main,* 2d ed. (London, 1860), 368. Trollope visited Bermuda as a civil servant charged with inspecting the postal system. In 1873 he met Clemens at the Garrick Club, in London, and in an autobiographical dictation in the summer of 1907, Clemens recalled Trollope "pouring forth a smooth and limpid and sparkling stream of faultless English"; see *Mark Twain in Eruption,* edited by Bernard DeVoto (New York, 1940), 333. Rudyard Kipling first encountered the scenery of the Islands in 1894. He, too, thought of Shakespeare. The artist Marsden Hartley, who sojourned in Bermuda in the winter of 1916–1917, wrote Alfred Stieglitz that life was so sluggish, "I know I should perish if I remained here a year"; see Townsend Ludington, *Marsden Hartley* (Boston, 1992), 134.

28. C. M. Allen to William H. Seward, May 31, 1867; see "Dispatches from United States Consuls in Bermuda, 1818–1906," the National Archives. Allen's reports were typically terse and routine, often nothing more than listings of fees, expenses, and ship arrivals.

29. Myra [Mary Mason Fairbanks], "Pilgrimizing," *Cleveland Herald,* December 14, 1867, 2. The festive opening of the Causeway on September 19, 1871, was proclaimed a "General Holiday and Day of Public Thanksgiving"; see the *Bermuda Royal Gazette* of that date. Much of the Causeway was destroyed by a hurricane in 1899. It was damaged again by Hurricane Fabian on September 5, 2003. Four persons in cars were swept off the pavement and drowned.

30. George Grove was trained as a civil engineer. In 1844 he supervised the construction of a cast-iron lighthouse on Morant Point in Jamaica. Bermuda stone was deemed not strong enough for the tall Gibbs Hill lighthouse, more than 105 feet from its base to the floor of the lantern; see *Lighthouses* (House of Commons, London, August 1, 1850), 104; and Michael Dolding, *Bermuda Light: The Story of Gibbs Hill Lighthouse* (Bermuda, n.d.), 31. A second lighthouse, on St. David's Island, was built of stone in 1876–1879. It stands only fifty-five feet from base to lantern. Gibbs Hill is named for Thomas Gibbs, scion of an old Bermuda family; see G. Daniel Blagg, *Bermuda Atlas & Gazetteer* (Dover, DE, 1997), 321.

31. *Journal Letters of Emily A. Severance: "Quaker City," 1867,* edited by Julia Severance Millikin (Cleveland, 1938), 208–13; Tom Reigstadt, "Harriet Langdon Albright, Olivia Clemens's Buffalo Cousin," *Mark Twain Society Bulletin* (January 1992): 1–3. For the latter citation, I am indebted to Jane McCone. Harriet Langdon, originally from Belmont, was a

sister of Julia Langdon—who, as Julia L. Langdon Barber, wrote Clemens on January 18, 1907, to ask if he would autograph the "Hillcrest Edition" of his works she was about to order from Harper Brothers. "This I particularly desire for *The Innocents Abroad,*" she wrote, "emphasizing the fact of my having been one of your favored listeners to the reading of the manuscript, upon the return voyage of the *Quaker City* via Bermuda."

32. W. C. J. Hyland Papers, Bermuda Archives, Hamilton.

33. *The Innocents Abroad,* 642; *Traveling with the Innocents Abroad: Mark Twain's Original Reports from Europe and the Holy Land,* edited by Daniel Morley McKeithan (Norman, OK, 1958), 311; Col. William R. Denny's journal, as quoted in Robert Hirst, "Sinners & Pilgrims," *Bancroftiana,* no. 113 (Fall 1998): 6; *The Innocents Abroad,* 644.

34. Autobiographical dictation of October 2, 1906, in *Mark Twain in Eruption,* 392; *The Innocents Abroad,* 640–41.

11. An Idle Excursion in 1877

1. Letter to John Russell Young, *Mark Twain's Letters,* vol. 2, edited by Harriet Elinor Smith and Richard Bucci (Berkeley, CA, 1990), 108.

2. *The Autobiography of Mark Twain,* ed. Charles Neider (New York, 1959), 41; *Mark Twain's Notebooks & Journals,* vol. 2, edited by Frederick Anderson, Lin Salamo, and Bernard L. Stein (Berkeley, CA, 1975), 9; *Adventures of Huckleberry Finn* (1885), 292; *What Is Man?* (1906), 27. Pangs of conscience, meaningful or not, constitute one of the most persistent themes in Clemens's life and work. Albert Bigelow Paine speaks of his "daily self-chidings" (*Mark Twain: A Biography,* 3 vols. [New York, 1912], 2:569).

3. *The Adventures of Tom Sawyer* (1876), 270; *A Tramp Abroad* (1880), 126; *The Gilded Age* (with Charles Dudley Warner, 1873), 545.

4. Leah A. Strong, *Joseph Hopkins Twichell, Mark Twain's Friend and Pastor* (Athens, GA, 1966), 68. "He is the prince of raconteurs," Twichell wrote ("Mark Twain," *Harper's New Monthly Magazine* [May 1896]: 820).

5. "In the Aid of the Blind," *Mark Twain's Speeches* (1910), 328. "I always travel with clergymen when I can," he said. "It is better for them, it is better for me. And any preacher who goes out with me in stormy weather and without a lightning rod is a good one."

6. *Mark Twain's Notebooks & Journals,* 2:12, 15–16, 30.

7. A. Emilius Outerbridge, "The New York Mail Steam Service, 1873–1884," *Bermuda Royal Gazette,* July 1, 1884. The first steamer on a mail line between Nassau and England had arrived on March 1, 1842, according to John J. Bushell (*Bushell's Handbook* [Hamilton, Bermuda, 1909], 47). A few steamships were sighted earlier. The *Bermuda Report, 2nd ed., 1985–1988* (Hamilton, Bermuda), states that tourists appeared as early as 1852 (126). In the *New York Times,* a correspondent identified only as "W. D." wrote, "We don't know much about Bermuda up in New York" (January 22, 1883, 2). Even today, many Americans confuse Bermuda with the Bahamas. Mark Twain refers to subsidies for mail steamships in a piece titled "The Case of George Fisher" (1871), in *Sketches, New and Old* (1875), 110n. For a detailed study of visitors to the Islands, see Duncan McDowall, *Another World: Bermuda and the Rise of Modern Tourism* (London, 1999).

8. Anthony Trollope, *The West Indies and the Spanish Main,* 2d ed. (London, 1860), 367, 370, 373. Julia C. R. Dorr wrote that "everybody is lazy in Bermuda, speaking from a New England point of view; but it is a very charming laziness" (*Bermuda: An Idyl of the Summer Islands* [New York, 1884], 61). In her article "Bermudian Days," she called the Islands a "lazy, lotus-eating land, where it seems always afternoon" (*Atlantic Monthly,* December 1883, 786).

9. "Sketches in Bermuda," *Harper's Weekly,* October 11, 1873, 901. Yellow fever had struck the garrison at St. George's in October 1867; see the *Illustrated London News,* December 28, 1867, 721. "A Cruise to the Somers Islands" mocked Bermuda as a "convict station" with some twelve hundred prisoners, and asserted that emancipation had been a failure because the colored population was slothful, immoral, dishonest, and so on (*Harper's Weekly,* March 21, 1857, 184–85). In *The Tempest,* Ariel tells Prospero that the Islands are still "vex'd" by storms (1.2). The Earl of Southampton, a patron of Shakespeare, was a shareholder in the Virginia Company and among those who in 1610 saw William Strachey's long report on the wreck of the *Sea Venture.*

10. The correction on November 8, 1873, in *Harper's Weekly* also apologizes to the citizens of Bermuda and admits that many of the unfavorable comments were "grossly inaccurate." Offprints of "Bermuda," the subsequent article by Christiana Rounds in *Harper's Monthly* (March 1874, 484–500), were distributed by the Quebec S. S. Company to well-to-do persons in the New York area.

11. Joseph H. Twichell journals, May 28, 1877, Beinecke Rare Book and Manuscript Library, Yale University, New Haven, CT; Archibald Henderson, "Mark Twain," *Harper's Monthly,* May 1909, 950. In the twentieth century, the journalist comparable to Mark Twain, surely, was A. J. Liebling of the *New Yorker,* a fact overlooked in the otherwise excellent essay by Russell Baker, "A Great Reporter at Large," *New York Review,* November 18, 2004, 12–16. The name "Youth" was understood by Clemens as gently satirical but affectionate. His wife always said he was the most difficult child she had; see *Chapters from My Autobiography* (1906–1907), 4:715, 7:1089.

12. The "Idle Excursion" first appeared in the *Atlantic Monthly,* October 1877, 443–47; November 1877, 586–92; December 1877, 718–24; and January 1878, 12–19. It also appeared in the *Canadian Monthly and National Review* and *Belgravia* (London), and was reprinted in the collections titled *Punch, Brothers, Punch!* (New York, 1878), *The Stolen White Elephant, Etc.* (Boston, 1882), and *Eighteen Short Stories and Sketches* (New York, 1892). Parts of the fourth article were published in the *Bermuda Royal Gazette,* April 2, 1878. The "Idle Excursion" nevertheless remains almost always out-of-print. The extracts used here, with elisions, appear in the original sequence and are taken from *The Stolen White Elephant, Etc.,* 36, 40–41, 61–74, 79–81, 85–94.

13. *Lady Brassey's Three Voyages in the Sunbeam* (London, 1886), pt. 3, 50. Hinson's Island in 1920 became the site of the first seaplane station in Bermuda; see Colin A. Pomeroy, *The Flying Boats of Bermuda* (Hamilton, Bermuda, 2000), 8–9.

14. Trollope, *West Indies,* 369; Rounds, "Bermuda," 489; *New York Times,* April 1, 1883, 3; James H. Stark, *Stark's Illustrated Bermuda Guide* (Boston, 1890), 12; Trollope, *West Indies,* 370. William Dean Howells described the houses of St. George as being of "Italian or

Spanish-American fancy" ("A Bermudan Sojourn," *Harper's Monthly Magazine,* December 1911, 16). Howells may have thought *Bermudan* correct, but *Bermudian* (as used by Clemens and the steamships) is the common usage. It also sounds better.

15. *Bermuda Royal Gazette,* May 29, 1877. Wil Onions, who died in 1959, was the principal architect of the city hall and Arts Centre in Hamilton (1958–1960), a leading exponent of traditional stone cottage design, and a founding partner of Onions, Bouchard & McCulloch (now OBM Limited). Mark Twain's words on onions appear typically exaggerated, but when an elderly woman from Spanish Point was asked recently whether she was a native Bermudian, she responded, "Yes, I'm an *onion.*"

16. *The Innocents Abroad,* 459–60, 626.

17. *New York Times,* April 15, 1883, 4. Regardless of the winter "season," Bermuda enjoys its best weather in the spring and fall.

18. *Mark Twain–Howells Letters,* edited by Henry Nash Smith and William M. Gibson, 2 vols. (Cambridge, MA, 1960), 1:389. One of Mark Twain's most condensed philosophical statements, the posthumously published "Macfarlane," is set in a boardinghouse; and in *No. 44, the Mysterious Stranger,* also published posthumously, a principal character is named "Doangivadam." Mrs. Kirkham's house stood between the northward arm of Dundonald Street (now Beacon Street) and Angle Street.

19. Paine refers to this passage in the notebook, but fails to mention Clemens's disbelief in the building costs (*Mark Twain: A Biography,* 2:591).

20. On the force of circumstance, see, for example, "'The Turning-Point of My Life'" (1910), in *Collected Tales,* 2:929–38. The classic study of the traditional Bermuda cottage is John S. Humphreys, *Bermuda Houses* (Boston, 1923). The older houses of Bermuda have "the unity, charm and simplicity of an architecture that is the unaffected expression and natural outcome of environment," Humphreys states in the preface.

21. In *Life on the Mississippi,* Mark Twain memorably recalls the Hannibal of his childhood as "the white town drowsing in the sunshine of a summer's morning" (63), but in *The Adventures of Tom Sawyer,* Hannibal serves as the model for "the poor little shabby village of St. Petersburg" (21). Clemens associated whiteness with the innocence of young girls and the purity of the Garden of Eden before Adam and Eve were cursed by a moral sense and the notion of original sin. Winslow Homer also showed a "fascination with the pure white of the houses," Helen A. Cooper notes in *Winslow Homer Watercolors* (New Haven, CT, 1986), 226. Homer achieved white by leaving the paper untouched by his brush.

22. "Editor's Easy Chair," *Harper's New Monthly Magazine,* June 1901, 147.

23. Mark Twain wrote in 1866 that he saw "millions of cats" in Hawaii (*Roughing It,* 455). Clemens's fondness for cats was well known. His mother took in strays, he said, and once had nineteen cats. Mark Twain devoted an entire chapter of *No. 44, the Mysterious Stranger* to a cat, and in *The Tragedy of Pudd'nhead Wilson* (1894) wrote: "A home without a cat—and a well-fed, well-petted and properly revered cat—may be a perfect home, perhaps, but how can it prove title?" (18).

24. Trinity Church, built in Hamilton between 1845 and 1883, was burned down by an arsonist. Construction of the present Cathedral of the Most Holy Trinity was begun in 1886 at the same site on Church Street. Neither building should be confused with Holy Trinity

Church, beautifully sited by the shore of Harrington Sound, below Mount Wyndham. Churches remain a dominant feature of the landscape and culture of Bermuda.

25. Construction of the Wesley Methodist Church, sited on Church Street near Parliament Street, had begun in the fall of 1876. It succeeded the Methodist Chapel at the head of Queen Street.

26. Letter of November 18, 1907, to Dorothy Quick; see John Cooley, ed., *Mark Twain's Aquarium* (Athens, Ga., 1991), 82–83. Also see the *Bermuda Pocket Almanack* (Hamilton, Bermuda, 1877), 141, and Christine Phillips-Watlington, *Bermuda's Botanical Wonderland* (London, 1996), 86. The most celebrated parade of royal palms stood on Crow Lane just east of Hamilton. Abstracted, the endearing shape of the royal palm appears today in the concrete lampposts of Hamilton.

27. "Editor's Easy Chair," 151; Dorr, *Bermuda,* 56. Today the creatures are commonly called garden spiders.

28. I am indebted to Wolfgang Sterrer, PhD, curator of the Bermuda Natural History Museum, for this surprisingly precise information.

29. See John Cox et al., *Life in Old Bermuda* (Bermuda, 1998), 48; and Phillips-Watlington, *Bermuda's Botanical Wonderland,* 100.

30. Trollope, *West Indies,* 371; Howells, "Editor's Study," *Harper's,* June 1894, 152. In *Roughing It,* Mark Twain objected to the sameness and melancholy of the evergreens in California (408). It was once a tradition in Bermuda to place in a wedding cake a tiny cedar tree, and to plant it after the cake was cut. The cedars killed in the epidemic were largely replaced by the tall, fluffy casuarina trees ("whistling pines") from Australia.

31. Joseph Gwilt, *The Encyclopaedia of Architecture,* rev. ed. (London, 1867), 638. Shutters have been utterly neglected by professional architectural historians. Mark Twain refers to shutters in "Personal Habits of the Siamese Twins" (1869), "A Ghost Story" (1870), and "Speech on Accident Insurance" (1874), all in *Sketches, New and Old* (1875), 210, 216, 230; "The 'Tournament' in A.D. 1870" (1870), in *Collected Tales,* 1:419; *Roughing It,* 336; "The Loves of Alonzo Fitz Clarence and Rosannah Ethelton" (1878), in *The Stolen White Elephant, Etc.,* 283; *A Tramp Abroad,* 315; *Life on the Mississippi,* 350; *A Connecticut Yankee in King Arthur's Court,* 294, 519; and in the unfinished *Tom Sawyer's Conspiracy,* in *Mark Twain's Hannibal, Huck & Tom,* edited by Walter Blair (Berkeley, CA, 1969), 180.

32. *Tom Moore's Bermuda Poems and Notes,* edited by William Zuill (Hamilton, Bermuda, n.d.), 37. In a ditty titled "Those Annual Bills" (1874), Mark Twain parodies Moore's poem "Those Evening Bells" (*Sketches, New and Old,* 62).

33. He evidently meant daily cosmopolitan newspapers. The *Royal Gazette* was then only a folded broadsheet of four unnumbered pages, and until January 1900 it was published only on Tuesdays. Dorr called it "a quaint little sheet" that could be read in twenty minutes, advertisements and all (*Bermuda,* 140).

III. Hints from the Notebook

1. *Mark Twain–Howells Letters,* edited by Henry Nash Smith and William M. Gibson, 2 vols. (Cambridge, MA, 1960), 1:165, 178. Less than a year after Clemens died, Howells

spent three months on the Islands, from January to April 1911. In "A Bermudan Sojourn," he wrote that "there is more beauty to the square foot in Bermuda than anywhere else in the world" (*Harper's,* December 1911, 16). Julia C. R. Dorr had written that voyaging to the Islands was difficult, but "beyond Purgatory lies Paradise" ("Bermudian Days," *Atlantic Monthly,* December 1883, 778). Howells modified her words when he wrote that "you cannot arrive in that paradise but by way of purgatory"—a saying often attributed to Mark Twain (27). It has been assumed, and wrongly, that Clemens and Howells visited the Islands together.

2. Joseph H. Twichell journals, May 28, 1877, Beinecke Rare Book and Manuscript Library, Yale University, New Haven, CT.

3. "From Bermuda," *Hartford Daily Courant,* May 29, 1877, 2.

4. Mark Twain outlines the qualities of good writing in *The Innocents Abroad,* 492; "Report to the Buffalo Female Academy" (1870), in *Collected Tales,* 1:408–11; *Roughing It,* 90; "Fenimore Cooper's Literary Offences" (1895), in *How to Tell a Story, and Other Essays* (1897), 93–116; and "William Dean Howells" (1906), in *Collected Tales,* 2:722–30.

5. *The Gilded Age,* 81; "How to Tell a Story" (1895), in *How to Tell a Story,* 3–12. "The Invalid's Story," which he altered slightly for a speech in Paris, in April 1879, reappeared in *The Stolen White Elephant, Etc., in Merry Tales,* and in *The $30,000 Bequest, and Other Stories.* "The Captain's Story" was republished in *Merry Tales* and in *The $30,000 Bequest.*

6. Mark Twain's early writings, so often sardonic and morbid, already displayed his disappointment in a human race composed of "reptiles" and "insects." The early work thus refutes the common and simplistic notion that his "dark" worldview came late in life and from anger over the deaths in his family and his own declining health. Note again that he surrounded the story of a happy holiday in Bermuda with a yarn about maneuvering for burial plots and a tale about the stench from a supposed corpse.

7. "Riley—Newspaper Correspondent" (1870), in *Sketches, New and Old,* 154. In *Roughing It,* he cited editorial writers whose "work is creative, and not a mere mechanical laying-up of facts, like reporting" (401); in "Miss Clapp's School" (1864), he described school compositions containing "rigid, uncompromising facts . . . rather than ornamental fancies" (*Collected Tales,* 1:64); and in *Chapters from My Autobiography,* he joked that "all through my life my facts have had a substratum of truth" (16:785).

8. Rudyard Kipling, *From Sea to Sea: Letters of Travel* (1899; repr., New York, 1923), 167, 180. Mark Twain said that as a young newspaperman he "let fancy get the upper hand of fact too often when there was a dearth of news" (*Roughing It,* 296). Samuel E. Moffett wrote that Mark Twain in San Francisco proved "not adapted to routine newspaper work" ("Mark Twain: A Biographical Sketch," in *The $30,000 Bequest,* 341).

9. *Royal Gazette,* February 6, 1883; *Bermuda Pocket Almanack* (1877), 139; *Lady Brassey's Three Voyages in the Sunbeam* (London, 1886), pt. 3, 53; Dorr, "Bermudian Days," 785–86; and Christiana Rounds, "Bermuda," *Harper's,* March 1874, 490.

10. "Editor's Study," *Harper's,* June 1894, 152.

11. Ibid., 151.

12. *The Innocents Abroad,* 554; Albert Bigelow Paine, *Mark Twain: A Biography,* 3 vols. (New York, 1912), 2:895; Moffett, "Mark Twain," 335, 338. In a letter of November 1896 to H. H. Rogers, Clemens wrote that his subscription books were mostly sold to the vast class

of "people who don't visit bookstores" (*Mark Twain's Correspondence with Henry Huttleston Rogers, 1893–1909,* edited by Lewis Leary [Berkeley, CA, 1969], 249).

13. *New York Times,* February 25, 1883, 4; March 25, 1883, 3. The other fine residence was Inglewood, the home of James H. Trimingham, in Paget Parish. Whitney resigned from his consular post in 1878, and died at Mont Clare in 1889.

14. Dorr, "Bermudian Days," 780.

15. Allen said nothing of Mark Twain's visit in his dispatches to the secretary of state, just as he reported in 1867 merely that the *Quaker City* had anchored in St. George's Harbor. At the time of his death, on December 24, 1888, he was the second-oldest member of the consular corps in point of service. During the war years, Allen's duties in protecting the interests of the United States were "particularly delicate," the *Royal Gazette* said on January 1, 1889, but he found that the climate alleviated his asthma, and stayed on.

16. *Letters from the Earth,* in *What Is Man? and Other Philosophical Writings,* edited by Paul Baender (Berkeley, CA, 1973), 407–8. Also see *Royal Gazette,* July 1, 1884. Mark Twain wrote earlier of "those poor unfortunates who feel that they have a genius for music, and who drive their neighbors crazy every night in trying to develop and cultivate it" ("A Touching Story of George Washington's Boyhood" [1864], in *The Celebrated Jumping Frog of Calaveras County, and Other Sketches* [1867], 139). In a letter of September 4, 1874, he described his study pavilion at Quarry Farm, near Elmira, New York, as situated "remote from *all noise.*"

17. *Mark Twain–Howells Letters,* 1:185.

iv. Thirty Years Later, 1907

1. *New York Times,* February 6, 1883, 3. Princess Louise was thirty-four when she arrived in Bermuda.

2. *New York Times,* January 28, 10. In all, "W. D." sent fourteen reports from Bermuda. The other twelve were published on January 22, 2; February 11, 9; February 25, 3–4; March 4, 3; March 11, 3; March 18, 3; March 25, 3; April 1, 3; April 8, 3; April 15, 4; April 22, 4; and April 29, 4.

3. *Royal Gazette,* February 6, April 10, 1883. The *Times* correspondent misidentified the house as "Ingleside" and its owner as "John" Trimingham. The house burned in 1933.

4. "Editor's Study," *Harper's,* June 1894, 150; "Editor's Easy Chair," *Harper's,* June 1901, 147, 149. Also see *Graphic,* August 9, 1890, 147.

5. *Mark Twain's Speeches* (1910), 427, 433; *Chapters from My Autobiography,* 21:691; letter evidently posted late in January 1907, to decline an invitation. "The pen is irksome to me," he said in August 1906. "I was born lazy, and dictating has spoiled me" (*Mark Twain in Eruption,* edited by Bernard DeVoto [New York, 1940], 198).

6. *Mark Twain Speaking,* edited by Paul Fatout (Iowa City, 1976), 526.

7. *Chapters from My Autobiography,* 15:676–77; William Dean Howells, *My Mark Twain* (New York, 1910), 96; "Mark Twain in White Amuses Congressmen," *New York Times,* December 8, 1906, 5.

8. Miss Lyon's changing status with Clemens and his family is discussed at length by Karen Lystra in *Dangerous Intimacy* (Berkeley, CA, 2004). Also see Jennifer L. Rafferty,

"'The Lyon of St. Mark': A Reconsideration of Isabel Lyon's Relationship to Mark Twain," *Mark Twain Journal* (Fall 1996): 43–55. Typescripts of Miss Lyon's date books and journals are in the Mark Twain Papers.

9. "Bermuda," *New York Herald,* December 30, 1906, magazine sec., 10. The *Bermudian,* newly added to the Quebec S.S. Company line of "royal mail steamers," first appeared in Bermuda on January 9, 1905. Clemens regularly read the *Herald* and the *Times,* among other papers. During the winter of 1906–1907, despite his "permanent bronchitis" and the advice of doctors, he had delayed going to Bermuda; see Albert Bigelow Paine, *Mark Twain: A Biography,* 3 vols. (New York, 1912), 3:1333. Instead, he was eager to play billiards on a new table given to him by Mrs. H. H. Rogers.

10. *Royal Gazette,* advertisement on January 20, 1885; also see *Royal Gazette,* December 23, 1884, and an advertisement in James H. Stark, *Stark's Illustrated Bermuda Guide* (Boston, 1890).

11. Dictation of January 6, 1907; see *Chapters from My Autobiography,* 21:696–97. Slight variations in punctuation appear in the typescript transcribed here. His use of "unvexed" is clearly a play on Shakespeare's "still-vex'd Bermoothes." May 24 was also Empire Day (now celebrated as "Bermuda Day.") Twichell, disguised as the character Harris, mentions Kirkham's *Grammar* in *A Tramp Abroad,* 222. Abraham Lincoln walked miles to get a copy.

12. Clemens devised a ploy for a banquet in New York on November 15, 1889, in which the speaker would be announced as "Mr. Samuel Langhorne" (*Mark Twain Speaking,* 247). "George Wilkinson" appears as a generic name in *The Innocents Abroad,* 451; "George Peters" in *Adventures of Huckleberry Finn,* chap. 11, and elsewhere.

13. *Royal Gazette,* January 12, 1907, 2. Clemens frequently joked about his incessant smoking. He called it his "pet vice." In "Answers to Correspondents" (1865), he wrote of "the appalling aggregate of happiness lost in a lifetime . . . from *not* smoking" (*The Celebrated Jumping Frog of Calaveras County, and Other Sketches,* 35). Clemens said he never had to learn to smoke because he "came into the world asking for a light" (*Collected Tales,* 2:149). In 1897, in Switzerland, he said he could buy "plenty good enough cigars" at five dollars a thousand or ten dollars a barrel (Albert Locher, "'This Is Paradise, Here,'" *Mark Twain Journal* [Fall 2002]: 11). As to white suits, Clemens acknowledged the vanity of enjoying being talked about. August Feldner, the narrator in the unfinished *No. 44, the Mysterious Stranger,* described himself as a natural boy who "longed to be conspicuous, and wondered at and talked about" (*Mark Twain's Mysterious Stranger Manuscripts,* edited by William M. Gibson [Berkeley, CA, 1969], 246).

14. Euphemia Young Bell, *Beautiful Bermuda* (New York, 1902), 100.

15. "More Health than He Needs," *New York Times,* January 10, 1907, 2.

16. Joseph H. Twichell journal for 1907, Beinecke Rare Book and Manuscript Library, Yale University, New Haven, CT, 156. On January 26, Clemens mailed a foul-worded poem to Twichell, saying "all the periodicals" had rejected it, and pretending it should be published in the *Hartford Courant.*

17. *Adventures of Huckleberry Finn,* 19.

18. The Cottage Hospital advertised that it admitted patients either gratuitously or on payment of a weekly sum. It was succeeded in 1920 by King Edward VII Memorial

Hospital, on Point Finger Road in Paget. Today the old hospital building at 19 Happy Valley Road is the headquarters for the Department of Corrections and Officers Training School. See J. Randolf Williams, *Care: 100 Years of Hospital Care in Bermuda* (Bermuda, 1994).

19. *The Papers of Woodrow Wilson,* edited by Arthur S. Link et al., 69 vols. (Princeton, NJ, 1966–1994), 17:5, 26. Also see Kenneth S. Lynn, "The Hidden Agony of Woodrow Wilson," *Wilson Quarterly* (Winter 2004): 59–92.

v. Riding in a Donkey Cart, 1908

1. *Following the Equator,* 482, 548. Benares, on the left bank of the Ganges in northeastern India, is now called Varanasi. Clemens had begun buying shares of Plasmon in 1900, and he wrote that one pound of Plasmon powder, a product extracted from waste milk, contained as much nutriment as sixteen pounds of "the best beef" (*Mark Twain's Correspondence with Henry Huttleston Rogers,* edited by Lewis Leary [Berkeley, CA, 1969], 439).

2. Francesca, the daughter of a wealthy businessman, lived to be ninety; see Doris Lanier, "Mark Twain's Georgia Angel Fish," *Mark Twain Journal* [Spring 1986]: 4–16.

3. William Dean Howells, *My Mark Twain* (New York, 1910), 76; *A Connecticut Yankee in King Arthur's Court,* 395; *Chapters from My Autobiography,* 6:968; letter of August 26, 1909, to Helene Picard. He wrote in 1885 that man was the most detestable of all creatures (and the only one possessed of malice), and said in 1896 that man ranked at the bottom of the evolutionary chain; see *What Is Man? and Other Philosophical Writings,* edited by Paul Baender (Berkeley, CA, 1973), 60, 81.

4. *Mark Twain–Howells Letters,* edited by Henry Nash Smith and William M. Gibson, 2 vols. (Cambridge, Mass., 1960), 2:841; "Mark Twain's 70th Birthday," supp. to *Harper's Weekly,* December 23, 1905, 1886; Archibald Henderson, *Mark Twain* (New York, 1912), xi.

5. *Evening Dispatch* (Edinburgh), June 20, 1907, 5; *Tribune* (London), July 13, 1907, 7.

6. Harvey, too, suffered from bronchitis, as well as asthma. He lived at 1 West Seventy-second Street, New York, and had made his fortune in street railways. Also see Clemens's letter of July 8, 1907, to Carlotta Welles, in *Mark Twain's Aquarium,* edited by John Cooley (Athens, GA, 1991), 42.

7. Mark Twain was so accomplished at feigning improvisation that Albert Bigelow Paine thought he told the dog story for the first time at the Players Club, "inventing it, I believe, as he went along" (*Mark Twain: A Biography,* 3 vols. [New York, 1912], 3:1413). In a dictation of October 10, 1907, Clemens spoke of the technique for giving a recited tale "the captivating naturalness of an impromptu narration." In his last public address, given on June 10, 1909, for Francesca's graduating class at St. Timothy's School in Catonsville, Maryland, he again told the dog story. He also used it for the coda to *Chapters from My Autobiography.*

8. *Mark Twain in Eruption,* edited by Bernard DeVoto (New York, 1940), 320; *Mark Twain Speaking,* edited by Paul Fatout (Iowa City, 1976), 606. He was telling a variation of the story already in his lecture season of 1871–1872. Also see Dorothy Quick, *Enchantment* (Norman, OK, 1961), 150–57; and the *New York Times,* January 12, 1908, 2:2. Howells had written in 1901 that he hated to see Mark Twain "eating so many dinners, and writing so few books" (*Mark Twain–Howells Letters,* 2:735n). The same phenomenon in Paris gave Roger Shattuck the title for his classic study of the avant-garde, *The Banquet Years* (New York, 1958).

9. Laura Stedman and George M. Gould, M.D., *Life and Letters of Edmund Clarence Stedman* (New York, 1910), 2:411.

10. Jonathan Swift, letter of September 29, 1725 (*Gulliver's Travels and Other Writings,* edited by Ricardo Quintana [New York, 1958], 514). At the end of chapter 6 in *Gulliver's Travels,* Swift describes his countrymen as "the most pernicious Race of little odious Vermin that Nature ever suffered to crawl upon the Surface of the Earth." Clemens, of course, did have his short list of "hated persons."

11. Elizabeth Wallace, "Bermuda Journal," Elizabeth Wallace Papers, Minnesota Historical Society Library, St. Paul, 2, 3. The journal comes close to the memoir she published in 1913, but is less coy and saccharine. Miss Wallace was born in Bogotá, where her father was a Presbyterian missionary. She was a graduate of Wellesley College. The opening ball of the Bermuda season had taken place on January 2 at the Hamilton Hotel, with dancing until midnight. Today the tourist season runs from about April 15 to November 1, as reflected in the schedule of ferryboats from Hamilton Harbor.

12. Elizabeth Wallace, *Mark Twain and the Happy Island,* (Chicago, 1913), 1, 4, 5.

13. *Following the Equator,* 611, 708. He also wrote of the "deep, rich Mediterranean splendor" of Lake Annecy, in "Aix-les-Bains" (1891), *Collected Tales,* 2:12.

14. *Opposite Ireland Island, Bermuda,* a painting now owned by the Masterworks Foundation of Bermuda. Homer produced about twenty watercolors in Bermuda. Some have been erroneously identified as views from the Bahamas. He visited Bermuda in the winter of 1899–1900, and again in 1901; see Helen A. Cooper, *Winslow Homer Watercolors* (New Haven, CT, 1986), 218–27.

15. Miss Wallace's perception that the angelfish were surrogate daughters, not make-believe grandchildren, is supported by Dorothy Quick, who recalled that "he would tell me that I reminded him of his own little girls" (*Enchantment,* 123).

16. *The Papers of Woodrow Wilson,* edited by Arthur S. Link et al., 69 vols. (Princeton, NJ, 1966–1994), 17:4, 607–8.

17. Mary Allen Hulbert, *The Story of Mrs. Peck: An Autobiography* (New York, 1933), 141. Mrs. Peck, divorced in 1912, reverted to her earlier name. William Dean Howells wrote in 1911 of "proud Paget, across the bay, where most of the best society dwells" ("A Bermudan Sojourn," *Harper's Monthly,* December 1911, 22). For the snobbish aspect of Paget, also see Andrew Trimingham, "All the Way to Crow Lane Side," *Bermudian* (May 1991): 10, 32–33.

18. "Answers to Correspondents" (1865), in *The Celebrated Jumping Frog of Calaveras County,* 36. Wilson later feared his letters to Mrs. Peck would be published, and in a statement that remained private until after his death in 1924 wrote that they disclosed "a passage of folly and gross impertinence in my life." He said he was deeply ashamed and repentant. "Neither in act nor even in thought was the purity or honor of the lady concerned touched or sullied," he wrote with characteristic piety (*Papers of Wilson,* 34:496–97).

19. *Papers of Wilson,* 17:609–10; *Royal Gazette,* February 1, 1908.

20. *Royal Gazette,* February 4, 1908.

21. Upton Sinclair, *American Outpost: A Book of Reminiscences* (New York, 1932), 197; also see *The Autobiography of Mark Twain,* edited by Charles Neider (New York, 1959), 121.

22. *Royal Gazette,* February 8, 1908; Sinclair, *Mammonart: An Essay in Economic Interpretation* (Pasadena, CA, 1925), 328. Sinclair recalled William Dean Howells as a "gracious

and kindly gentleman," but a man who espoused the virtues and charms of a "middle-class gentility" and remained reluctant to put any trace of social protest into his magazine editing or writing (334–35).

23. Wallace, *Mark Twain and the Happy Island,* 12–15.

24. Paine, *Mark Twain: A Biography,* 3:1440–41. Van Gogh once remarked, "The world is a picture of God's that turned out badly."

25. *Royal Gazette,* February 8, 1908. The item in the *Gazette,* which said Mark Twain sailed "yesterday" (Friday, February 7), clearly represented type held over from the edition of Tuesday, February 4. Miss Wallace's journal notes (36) that the *Bermudian* was to have sailed at ten o'clock Monday morning, but was delayed and sailed instead at four that afternoon. Headed toward Bermuda on Sunday, February 2, the ship encountered the *Mary C. Newhall,* a four-masted cargo schooner disabled by storms and drifting. After a failed attempt Sunday night, six crew members from the *Bermudian* rescued the ten-man crew of the schooner early Monday morning.

vi. The Grand Return

1. Julia C. R. Dorr, "Bermudian Days," *Atlantic Monthly,* December 1883, 780; William Dean Howells, "Editor's Easy Chair," *Harper's Monthly,* June 1901, 148. Lady Brassey saw angelfish in a pond on Ireland Island, and found them "quite the most ethereal-looking objects I ever saw in this prosaic world of ours" (*Lady Brassey's Three Voyages in the Sunbeam* [London, 1886], pt. 3, 51. Once relished as table food, angelfish still symbolize Bermuda and appear on five-cent pieces, which the woodworker Cyril S. Smith regularly embeds in cedar paperweights for the tourist trade.

2. John S. Gregory, "Henry H. Rogers—Monopolist," *World's Work,* May 1905, 6128. "Business with him is war," Gregory wrote. Rogers was "delightfully free from hypocrisy," George Harvey wrote in *Harper's Weekly* (May 29, 1909, 5), shortly after the monopolist died. Rogers is also remembered for his large benefactions to Fairhaven, Massachusetts, his birthplace, where he improved even the streets.

3. *Mark Twain's Speeches,* 431. In 1897 he had dedicated *Following the Equator* to Harry Rogers (H. H. Rogers Jr.) "with recognition of what he is, and apprehension of what he may become, unless he form himself a little more closely upon the model of The Author."

4. *New York Times,* February 23, 1908, 1. Mark Twain had written in 1903 that he "was never particular about the kind of people" with whom he kept company; see his self-interview, "Mark Twain, Able Yachtsman," *Collected Tales,* 2:558.

5. Elizabeth Wallace, *Mark Twain and the Happy Island* (Chicago, 1913), 44, 76; Wallace, *The Unending Journey* (Minneapolis, 1952), 159–60.

6. *Mark Twain's Speeches,* 32; William Dean Howells, *My Mark Twain* (New York, 1910), 5. "If ever a writer was imprisoned in his boyhood, clearly Mark Twain was," Bernard DeVoto comments in *Mark Twain at Work* (Cambridge, MA, 1942), 49n.

7. *Royal Gazette,* March 7, 1908. A few years later, Howells said of Front Street that "of all the commercial streets of the world, it seems to me the fairest" ("A Bermudan Sojourn," *Harper's Monthly,* December 1911, 22).

8. Elizabeth Wallace, "Bermuda Journal," Elizabeth Wallace Papers, Minnesota Historical Society Library, St. Paul, 49; Marion Schuyler Allen, "Our Friend, Mark Twain," typed manuscripts in various versions, Allen Collection, Bermuda Archives, Hamilton. Mrs. Allen later published a shortened and edited text, "Some New Anecdotes of Mark Twain," *Strand Magazine* (London), August 1913, 166–72. I have relied on the several manuscript versions. Clemens thought the Standard Oil Trust was unfairly prosecuted by the government over a "quibble," and said President Theodore Roosevelt, carrying the "Big Stick" and ever alert to popular approval, had become the most formidable disaster in American history since the Civil War (*Mark Twain in Eruption,* edited by Bernard DeVoto [New York, 1940], 16–18).

9. Wallace, "Bermuda Journal," 80; Albert Bigelow Paine, *Mark Twain: A Biography,* 3 vols. (New York, 1912), 3:1208; Rudyard Kipling, *From Sea to Sea* (New York, 1923), 170–71. Helen Keller, whose training was financed by H. H. Rogers, and who had met Mark Twain when she was a child, found his voice truly amazing. "To my touch, it was deep, resonant," she wrote. "He had the power of modulating it so as to suggest the most delicate shades of meaning and he spoke so deliberately that I could get almost every word with my fingers on his lips" (*Midstream: My Later Life* [New York, 1929], 66–67). Clemens considered her the most wonderful woman since Joan of Arc. He admired Kipling's ballads, despite his distaste for the idea of "the White Man's burden" in uplifting the presumably sullen natives. Kipling stayed three weeks at the Hamilton Hotel in 1894, and visited the Islands again from March to June 1930, staying first in the Bermudiana Hotel and then in a private guesthouse; see Eileen Stamers-Smith, "Kipling and Bermuda," *Bermuda Journal of Archaeology and Maritime History* (1996): 100–114.

10. *Royal Gazette,* March 31, 1908.

11. Wallace, *Mark Twain and the Happy Island,* 75. Also see the *Royal Gazette,* December 31, 1907; "The Bermuda Aquarium," *Zoological Society Bulletin* (New York) (April 1909): 481–84; Louis S. Mowbray, "The World's Finest Marine Exhibit," *Empire Digest* (October 1944): 44–48; and "Bermuda Aquarium, the First Ten Years," *Critter Talk* (Flatts, Bermuda) (Fall 1980): 2–3. Louis S. Mowbray (1909–1976), the son of Louis L. Mowbray (1877–1952), was also a naturalist.

12. *St. Louis Post-Dispatch,* March 8, 1908.

13. For accounts of the performance in Bermuda, see "Samuel Langhorne Clemens (1835–1910)," *Bermuda Historical Quarterly* (Autumn 1977): 58–59; and the *Royal Gazette,* March 7, 1908.

14. *Following the Equator,* 167; *How to Tell a Story, and Other Essays,* 4. In his tale about the jumping frog, Mark Twain wrote of a narrator who never smiled or showed any awareness of anything ridiculous or funny about the story (*The Celebrated Jumping Frog of Calaveras County, and Other Sketches,* 8–9). It was a trait Clemens learned from his mother.

15. Miss Wallace was so impressed by Gay's courteous letter that she asked permission to copy it. She quoted parts in *Mark Twain and the Happy Island,* 65–66, and later reproduced the letter in *The Unending Journey,* 163–64. The *Cressy,* as she noted, was sunk in the North Sea by a German submarine in World War I. As if to forecast Mark Twain, the earlier John Gay (1685–1732) had asked Alexander Pope to see that his gravestone read: "Life is a Jest, and all Things show it; I thought so once, but now I know it."

16. See *Royal Gazette,* January 11, 1908. Miss Wallace obviously erred in *Mark Twain and the Happy Island* when she asserted that Clemens "showed no interest in crystal caves, nor natural bridges, nor coral gardens" (70). Still privately owned and operated commercially, the Crystal Cave now has eighty-one steps.

17. *The Adventures of Tom Sawyer,* 254; Albert Bigelow Paine, "The Boy Cave-Finder of Bermuda," *St. Nicholas* (March 1911): 447–51; Henry C. Wilkinson, *The Adventurers of Bermuda,* 2d ed. (London, 1958), 22–23. In 1945 an American airman jogging on Coopers Island discovered bird bones and a freshly killed specimen that he and a friend preserved. Later, at the Smithsonian Institution, it was identified as a cahow. Living cahows were discovered again in 1951; see the *Royal Gazette,* October 24, 2003, 5. Wolfgang Sterrer notes that the cahow, the only endemic bird on the Islands, is nocturnal and subterranean when on land, and rears its chick in a burrow (*Bermuda's Marine Life* [Bermuda, 1992], 281–82).

18. *Royal Gazette,* March 31, 1908. He inscribed the same words on books he gave to other schoolgirls.

19. *New York Times,* April 19, 1908, 6:4.

20. The ingredients of West Indian pepper pot are given in Carveth Wells, *Bermuda in Three Colors* (New York, 1935), 256.

21. Marion Schuyler was married in New York City to William H. Allen, a native of Belmont, New York (see *New York Times,* October 26, 1892, 4; and the *Royal Gazette,* November 8, 1892). At first they lived at Wistowe, in Flatts, where Helen was born September 6, 1894. Bay House on Cockle Point was originally a small cottage that faced Pitt's Bay. It should not be confused with the Bay House in Hamilton Parish, on Bailey's Bay, or the Bay House at the northwest end of St. David's Island, in St. George's Parish.

22. *New York Times,* April 19, 1908, 6:4, *The Adventures of Tom Sawyer,* 109–11. Also see *Chapters from My Autobiography,* 5:841–42. A pictorial feature headed "Well-Known Men in Their Hours of Recreation" in the *New York Times* illustrated such pursuits as golf, croquet, fishing, and sailing, but showed Mark Twain seated and holding a cat (August 16, 1908, 5).

23. *Royal Gazette,* April 4, 1908.

24. *The Tragedy of Pudd'nhead Wilson,* 179. Among his vivid recollections of life on his uncle's farm, Mark Twain states: "I know the taste of the watermelon which has been honestly come by, and I know the taste of the watermelon which has been acquired by art. Both taste good, but the experienced knows which tastes best" (*Chapters from My Autobiography,* 13:461). He once wrote Rogers, "I haven't had anything that tasted so good, since stolen watermelon" (*Mark Twain's Correspondence with Henry Huttleston Rogers,* edited by Lewis Leary [Berkeley, CA, 1969], 592).

25. *Royal Gazette,* April 11, 1908; *Mark Twain: Plymouth Rock and the Pilgrims, and Other Speeches,* edited by Charles Neider (New York, 1984), 321–27. The stolen watermelon story had been in his repertoire many years. Stolen watermelons also figure in *The Adventures of Tom Sawyer,* 180; and *Adventures of Huckleberry Finn,* 95, 310.

26. *New York Times,* April 14, 1908, 9. Bermuda had been a source of specimen fish for many years; in September 1877, for instance, a ship carried eighteen angelfish, an octopus, a sand shark, a green moray eel, and other specimens to New York. Castle Clinton, built as a fort in 1807, was remodeled by the architects McKim, Mead, and White as the new aquar-

ium, and opened in December 1896. As an Easter gift, Dorothy Sturgis sent Clemens a sketch she had made of the "Unfinished Church" in St. George's Parish, still a tourist sight (*Mark Twain's Aquarium,* edited by John Cooley [Athens, GA, 1991], 143).

27. The letter is quoted in his autobiographical dictation of April 17, 1908. He spelled Helen Martin's given name either as "Helen" or "Hellen."

28. Dorothy Quick, *Enchantment* (Norman, OK, 1961), 167.

VII. On Doctor's Orders, 1909

1. [Neltje DeGraff Doubleday], "Stormfield, Mark Twain's New Country Home," *Country Life in America,* April 1909, 608. Mrs. Doubleday, the wife of Frank N. Doubleday of Doubleday, Page, and Company, publisher of that magazine and others, wrote books about birds, nature, and the American Indian. In 1906 her husband arranged for the anonymous publication of *What Is Man?* because of Mark Twain's overriding reputation as a humorist. Clemens had complained in 1874 of being bothered all day by so many details in the finishing of his house in Hartford. Miss Lyon suggested the name "Autobiography House" as early as August 1906. On the day Clemens first saw the new house he pronounced it perfect, and said, "It might have been here always" (Albert Bigelow Paine, "Mark Twain at Stormfield," *Harper's Monthly Magazine,* May 1909, 957). He also wrote William Dean Howells that the house was "John's triumph." Clemens tried to get the elder Howells to build a house nearby, just as he had invited him in 1874 to move from Cambridge, Massachusetts, to Hartford.

2. For differing accounts of these late years, see Karen Lystra, *Dangerous Intimacy* (Berkeley, CA, 2004); and Hamlin Hill, *Mark Twain, God's Fool* (New York, 1973).

3. *Harper's Monthly,* December 1907, 41–49; January 1908, 266–76. Paine's letter of November 6, 1910, to Mrs. Allen, and Clara Clemens's letter of December 21, 1910, are in the Allen Collection, Bermuda Archives, Hamilton.

4. Elizabeth Wallace, *Mark Twain and the Happy Island* (Chicago, 1913), 105–6. Albert Bigelow Paine slightly misdates the incident of Clemens's dizziness (*Mark Twain: A Biography,* 3 vols. [New York, 1912], 3:1458–59). Miss Lyon's date book shows it to have occurred ten days earlier, or late in July.

5. Paine, "Mark Twain at Stormfield," 957.

6. Letter of February 6, 1861, to Orion Clemens.

7. *What Is Man? and Other Philosophical Writings,* edited by Paul Baender (Berkeley, CA, 1973), 406–11, 417, 425, 428, 443. *Letters from the Earth* remained unpublished until 1962. Mark Twain wrote a tale in 1869 about a fortune-teller saying he would be condemned to hang and would undergo conversion, after which "the best and purest young ladies of the village will assemble in your cell and sing hymns" (*Collected Tales,* 1:326).

8. *Mark Twain–Howells Letters,* edited by Henry Nash Smith and William M. Gibson, 2 vols. (Cambridge, MA, 1960), 2:848. An 1873 advertisement for *Roughing It* said the book was "related in his own style, which if in no other way meritorious, is at least an original one."

9. *The Adventures of Tom Sawyer,* 21; "The New Planet," *Collected Tales,* 2:875–76. The

unseen planet was finally discovered in 1930, and given the name Pluto to honor Percival Lowell by using his initials. Mark Twain had written in *The Innocents Abroad* of the pride and delight in discovery (266), and in *What Is Man?* of an astronomer who "infers an invisible planet" (94).

10. Paine, *Mark Twain: A Biography,* 3:1543. Paine mistakenly wrote that they had sailed on November 19 rather than on Saturday, November 20.

11. Lefroy's compendium, published in 1877–1879, is now greatly supplemented by A. C. Hollis Hallett, ed., *Bermuda under the Sommer Islands Company 1612–1684 Civil Records,* 3 vols. (Bermuda, 2005).

12. *Collected Tales,* 2:937–38. The essay first appeared in *Harper's Bazar,* February 1910. In a speech delivered in London more than thirty-five years earlier, Mark Twain had been pleased to quote two verses by Isaac Watts, the English minister: "Let dogs delight to bark and bite, / For God hath made them so" (*Mark Twain's Speeches,* 97). And in an autobiographical dictation on September 4, 1907, he emphasized that there was "no such thing as free will in the composition of any human being that ever lived."

13. Paine, *Mark Twain: A Biography,* 3:1544–45.

14. *New York Times,* December 21, 1909, 1. The *Royal Gazette* on Tuesday, December 21, said Clemens and Paine were sailing that morning from Bermuda; clearly, the item had been held over from Saturday, December 18.

VIII. Islands of the Blest, 1910

1. Alexander Pope, "Epistle to Dr. Arbuthnot" (1735), verse 132. The autobiographical dictation is dated December 24, 1909. Jane Lampton (Jean) Clemens died at twenty-nine. Her sister Olivia Susan (Susy) Clemens died in 1896 at twenty-four. Their brother, Langdon Clemens, died in 1872 at nineteen months. Mark Twain said repeatedly that death was life's greatest prize. He once wrote in a notebook: "Stingy Nature gives us only one valuable gift which she does not take away from us again—death."

2. Paine's letters to Mr. and Mrs. Allen are in the Allen Collection, Bermuda Archives, Hamilton.

3. One of the anomalies of Clemens's character resided in his deeply skeptical regard for human nature in combination with a naive optimism when he invested in perilous business propositions.

4. William Dean Howells, *My Mark Twain* (New York, 1910), 100–101, 108, 111. Howells had become America's leading man of letters. He held that Mark Twain was "the Lincoln of our literature" (101).

5. His letter of January 11, 1910, appears in *Mark Twain's Letters,* edited by Albert Bigelow Paine (New York, 1917), 2:837–38. Clemens's concern over a previous encounter with Governor Kitchener was typical of his politeness. Kitchener served as governor from November 1908 until his death in March 1912 in the military hospital at Prospect.

6. Although the final paragraph in this letter of January 18, 1910, seems uncharacteristically insensitive, it accords with the attitude Mark Twain expressed in such phrases as "the encumbering flesh" and "these bonds of flesh—this decaying vile matter . . . this loathsome

sack of corruption in which my spirit is imprisoned" (*Mark Twain's Mysterious Stranger Manuscripts,* edited by William M. Gibson [Berkeley, CA, 1969], 343, 369).

7. Clemens in the 1880s described the Sandwich Islands as the "isles of the blest" (Albert Bigelow Paine, *Mark Twain: A Biography,* 3 vols. (New York, 1912), 1:714, 879.

8. Miss Wallace elided the stronger parts of this letter in her memoir, *Mark Twain and the Happy Island* (Chicago, 1913), 137. Clemens said he had furnished his children with "worldly knowledge and wisdom, but was not competent to go higher, and so left their spiritual education in the hands of the mother" (*Chapters from My Autobiography,* 14:562). Elsewhere in his autobiography he remarked that he took "no interest in otherworldly things," and was convinced that "we know nothing whatever about them and have been wrongly and uncourteously and contemptuously left in total ignorance of them" (*Mark Twain in Eruption,* edited by Bernard DeVoto [New York, 1940], 339).

9. "Editor's Easy Chair," *Harper's Monthly,* March 1918, 603; also see William Dean Howells, "Mr. Harben's Georgia Fiction," *North American Review* (March 1910): 359; and *Mark Twain–Howells Letters,* edited by Henry Nash Smith and William M. Gibson, 2 vols. (Cambridge, MA, 1960), 2:852. In *Following the Equator,* at the head of chapter 12, Mark Twain states: "There are those who scoff at the schoolboy, calling him frivolous and shallow. Yet it was the schoolboy who said 'Faith is believing what you know ain't so.'" Clemens's notes on Harben seem like section 45 of *The Antichrist,* but Miss Lyon said he expressed little interest in Nietzsche. In *Mark Twain's Mysterious Stranger Manuscripts,* the protagonist says the "hysterically insane" universe and its contents can only be "dreams, visions, fictions!" (404).

10. Woodrow Wilson, *The Papers of Woodrow Wilson,* edited by Arthur S. Link et al., 69 vols. (Princeton, NJ, 1966–1994), 20:133.

11. "Mark Twain at Bermuda," *Human Life* (Boston) (May 1910): 15, 40; reprinted in *Mark Twain Journal* (Spring 2000): 10–12. The writer remains obscure. "Mildred Champagne" was a pseudonym used by two elderly men who conducted a daily column in the *Boston Post* headed "Talks on Love and Sentiment." They took turns inventing questions from the imaginary lovelorn and providing advice; see the *Christian Science Monitor,* January 11, 2002, 23. But the reporter who interviewed Mark Twain after invading the grounds of Bay House, wrote Mrs. Allen, was a woman who had gone "so far as to push herself into the privacy of his very bed-room where he was lying down."

12. "The Great Dark," *Collected Tales,* 2:341.

13. Dorothy Quick, *Enchantment* (Norman, OK, 1961), 213.

14. The letter notably echoes and amplifies the same feelings about Bermuda he expressed after his "idle excursion" with Twichell in 1877.

15. "Mark Twain," *North American Review* (July 5, 1907): 542, 548. Phelps taught at Yale for forty-one years. He was only thirteen and a pupil at the Hartford West Middle Grammar School in April 1878 when Mark Twain spoke on Methuselah to the graduating class. The thrust of the talk was that 20 years of modern American life were longer and richer than the 969 years of the patriarch.

16. Clemens in writing Phelps referred to Bermuda as "this little paradise." In *Following the Equator,* Mark Twain mentioned the Sandwich Islands, "which to me were Paradise"

(48). The angry remarks to Miss Wallace were omitted, again, in the "Letters" section of her 1913 memoir. The narrator in *Mark Twain's Mysterious Stranger Manuscripts* enjoys a "gush of thankfulness" when told there is no afterlife (404).

17. Howard G. Baetzhold and Joseph B. McCullough, ed., *The Bible according to Mark Twain* (Athens, GA, 1995), app. 1, 271.

18. *New York Times,* March 22, 1910, 9. Collier, head of the publishing house, wrote Clemens in 1908 that he was sending a baby elephant to Stormfield as a Christmas gift. First, bales of hay and bushels of carrots arrived, then the elephant—a toy only two feet long. "It was a very successful joke," Clemens wrote Dorothy Quick a week after Christmas.

19. The witty response from Clemens proved he was as alert as ever, contrary to latter-day commentary.

20. Much earlier, around 1881, he had satirized books on etiquette; see "Etiquette," *Collected Tales,* 1:786–800.

21. For this vague and thirdhand report, see Hamlin Hill, *Mark Twain, God's Fool* (New York, 1973), 261; and Laura E. Skandera-Trombley, *Mark Twain in the Company of Women* (Philadelphia, 1994), 182.

Index

Numbers in italics refer to illustrations. SC=Samuel Clemens.